DECODING BLOCKCHAIN FOR BUSINESS

UNDERSTAND THE TECH AND PREPARE FOR THE BLOCKCHAIN FUTURE

Stijn Van Hijfte

Apress®

Decoding Blockchain for Business: Understand the Tech and Prepare for the Blockchain Future

Stijn Van Hijfte
Ghent, Belgium

ISBN-13 (pbk): 978-1-4842-6136-1   ISBN-13 (electronic): 978-1-4842-6137-8
https://doi.org/10.1007/978-1-4842-6137-8

Copyright © 2020 by Stijn Van Hijfte

Managing Director, Apress Media LLC: Welmoed Spahr
Acquisitions Editor: Shiva Ramachandran
Development Editor: Matthew Moodie
Coordinating Editor: Rita Fernando

Cover designed by eStudioCalamar

Distributed to the book trade worldwide by Springer Science+Business Media New York, 1 New York Plaza, New York, NY 100043. Phone 1-800-SPRINGER, fax (201) 348-4505, e-mail orders-ny@springer-sbm.com, or visit www.springeronline.com. Apress Media, LLC is a California LLC and the sole member (owner) is Springer Science + Business Media Finance Inc (SSBM Finance Inc). SSBM Finance Inc is a **Delaware** corporation.

For information on translations, please e-mail booktranslations@springernature.com; for reprint, paperback, or audio rights, please e-mail bookpermissions@springernature.com.

Apress titles may be purchased in bulk for academic, corporate, or promotional use. eBook versions and licenses are also available for most titles. For more information, reference our Print and eBook Bulk Sales web page at http://www.apress.com/bulk-sales.

Any source code or other supplementary material referenced by the author in this book is available to readers on GitHub via the book's product page, located at www.apress.com/9781484261361. For more detailed information, please visit http://www.apress.com/source-code.

Printed on acid-free paper

For my beautiful wife-to-be, Tatiana

Contents

About the Author

Stijn Van Hijfte has experience as a consultant, lecturer, and an innovation officer and has worked over the years with cloud, AI, automation, and blockchain technologies. Since 2015, he has been experimenting and exploring with the blockchain space, gaining deeper insight into the entire ecosystem, from setting up nodes and writing smart contracts, to the legal implications of GDPR, ICOs, and cryptocurrencies. Among others, he holds degrees in economics, IT, and data science. He currently works at Deloitte as a Senior Consultant and as a lecturer at Howest Applied University College.

Acknowledgments

There are several people I want to thank for this book. This certainly wasn't an endeavor I started alone, so a lot of people deserve to be mentioned here (sorry if I skipped you!)

I first want to thank the people of Apress publishing. This was my first book, and they met me with enthusiasm and were eager to help me every step of the way. A special thanks to Shiva, who was the first to offer me positive feedback and lead me through the process. Thanks also to Rita and Matthew, who helped me review and adapt the book to what it is today. Even in difficult times, they were more than willing to help me every step of the way.

I would also like to thank some people who are special to me. I would like to thank my parents. They have always supported me throughout my life, no matter what. My father taught me the value of perseverance and that I should never give up. Hard work eventually pays off. My mother gifted me with the passion for reading and learning, helping me every step of the way. She has always believed in me. Mom, dad, I love you.

I also want to thank my brother. He always keeps me on my toes and challenges me in everything. I can say that, without a doubt, he is always in my corner and forces me to look at things with a different perspective. If there is one person who always tells me the truth, even when I don't want to hear it, it is him. Bram, I couldn't have wished for a better brother and I can simply say that I love you (even if you don't want to hear it).

Of course, there is also my girlfriend (and wife-to-be), Tatiana. I dedicated this book to you for a reason. I have never been happier since I met you. I know I drive you crazy all the time, certainly when I am writing or babbling on about technical things. Thank you for putting up with me and challenging me every day (and I really mean every day) to do new things. And in case you might have missed it: I love you!

Finally, I would like to thank my friends and colleagues who have put up with me and my insanities over the years. I am the luckiest guy on the planet to have a group of people like you in my life. Some of you I have known for many years, and I thank you for being in my life. For those of you I have only recently met: you can stop dreaming, I never change. And one last special thanks to Karine Verstricht for the photo she made for the book!

Introduction

Hi. Yes, you. If you are reading this I assume you have heard about *blockchain* and would like to know more about the subject. Perhaps you had some cryptocurrencies in the past, heard the whispers about Bitcoin or other networks and are wondering if you should invest or not. You might have smirked at those who were investing in crypto and now are still "HODLing," as they like to call it, hoping that the value will go up to where it once was. Now you want to know what all the talk is actually about. Perhaps you heard about a possible project that could encapsulate blockchain technology. Or you might even have heard the question "do you believe in blockchain?" as if it were some kind of new religion.

Well, if you are looking to get some deeper understanding of what blockchain technology is and how it might impact your life, don't look any further. When we talk about blockchain, more often than not business professionals do not have a clear view on what has already been done with this new technology or what is going to happen in the near future. To lift the veil, this book will introduce blockchain to business professionals, specifically focusing on not just what blockchain is but how it's changing different industries.

We'll look at different major sectors to see how this technology is no longer something obscure and difficult to understand and use, but instead offers a new way of working and redesigning current, often terribly designed, processes. Blockchain holds the power to change platforms entirely so that competitors can work together in a trustless environment. This way, entire industries can be further optimized while at the same time improving the situation for their customers. I will not try to convince you or make you "believe" in anything. My goal is to provide a clear message about what blockchain is, how it is being applied, and what the possible legal and business opportunities are. What you do with this information is completely up to you. Why? It is only you, with the knowledge that you have acquired, who can determine if blockchain (or distributed ledgers for that matter) is for you. It will be up to you to determine if you can do something with this knowledge and change the world around you. If you don't, there is no judgment. And if you do, this book will hopefully help you make the right decisions. Of course, because I am the author of this book, you can rightly assume that I think positively of the blockchain technology. If some of the passages in the book sound a bit too optimistic in your opinion, I apologize. Again, it is not my goal to convince you of anything, merely to share information with you.

Some of you might be very skeptical. The cryptocurrency crash of 2019 is still fresh in many people's minds and somewhat tempered the optimistic potential people felt for blockchain originally. Some people think the technology has failed and that we should look to more traditional solutions. The truth is as always somewhere in the middle. As you will soon learn, the crash happened because of specific reasons. It might even be a good thing that the crash happened. It allows us to build a future based on more realistic terms, rather than dreaming of a completely new world tomorrow. As most of you know, the world doesn't change over night, and we shouldn't push for that either. Rather, we should use the tools and knowledge that is handed to us, and do the best we can to make a better world tomorrow, even by changing it a little bit. While we progress through these pages, you will understand how distributed ledgers could change the present as well as the future.

In this book, I cover some notable implementations of blockchain that show its potential but also the difficulties of the technology. A question that always must be asked is this: do we have to use distributed ledger/blockchain technology? Or even better: what is the added value of using blockchain? You might be able to use it, but you should do so only when it is beneficial to the project and organization, not just because it is blockchain? Sadly, this question is sometimes overlooked by people and companies that really want to join the hype but do not understand the underlying consequences of those choices.

As you will soon learn, blockchain technology requires a new way of thinking. Only when all the partners share this same view can a blockchain project succeed. One of the most annoying questions relating to blockchain is "how can we get the most benefit out of this?" This might be hard to understand at this moment, but distributed ledgers allow for competitors to cooperate to the benefit of all.

We'll also look into how blockchain technology affects other booming topics such as AI, IoT, and RPA. Emerging technologies aren't separate evolutions within our society but can easily combined into new solutions. These solutions can lead to even greater change and broader impact (or even greater disaster when done poorly).

We will also look at the influence of blockchain technology on the finance departments within major companies and on regulations surrounding blockchain. Finally, we'll end with some insights into cryptocurrencies. And now, let's begin the journey!

Blockchain in Business

A Short Word on the Past

While we are looking toward the future in this book, it is still crucial for you to understand the past. There have been some "experiments" in the past, such as *B-money*, which was a type of cryptocurrency released in 1998 by Wei Dai. (Bitcoin was even named after B-money, so its importance cannot be underestimated.) Even before the emergence of B-money, David Chaum created *ecash* in 1983. People often have the idea that the search for a real "digital" currency is something new, but ever since the advent of the Internet, people have been searching for ways to implement digital currencies securely. It is in this pursuit that blockchain finds its roots. Technologies rooted in security (such as hashcash) and the idea of peer-to-peer networks (which we know from file sharing applications such as Napster and BitTorrent) all also crucial parts that eventually led to the blockchain technology.

The real name of the person who started the entire blockchain revolution remains to this day unknown. All we know is that she/he/they called themselves "Satoshi Nakamoto." It was in 2008 that Satoshi Nakamoto published a whitepaper titled: "Bitcoin: A Peer-to-Peer Electronic Cash System." In this paper, an alternative solution was proposed to solve the well-known Byzantine General's problem in computer science and the double spending problem more known in economic fields. The Byzantine General's problem refers to

© Stijn Van Hijfte 2020
S. Van Hijfte, *Decoding Blockchain for Business*,
https://doi.org/10.1007/978-1-4842-6137-8_1

the issue of how one can know if a certain message is real when several parties are sending messages and one or more has become corrupted. Who do we trust and how do we know who the liar is? The double spending problem is a classic case surrounding digital currency. Physical money can only be spent once, but how do you prevent digital money from being spent twice?

In combination with earlier technologies, Satoshi Nakamoto introduced a new concept: a *proof-of-work algorithm* that would allow a distributed computer system to accept transactions in contrast to all earlier solutions, which needed, in one way or another, a central authority to accept transactions or create currency. Consensus is at the core of the paper; consensus between the members of the network. The main idea that you should consider when you think about the advent of blockchain is that of distrust. Bitcoin was created in a time of political and financial unrest, as the financial crisis of 2008 was unfolding all over the world. This distrust was of any central entity that could be corrupted or become "too big to fail." Blockchain could fix this very problem, as its entire system is built on not trusting the other party. You don't have to trust them and you don't need some impartial third party to validate the other participants. The network itself ensures that each participant falls in line, or is eventually destroyed by the network. That last statement might sound a little bit harsh, but it is a core concept to understand.

It was a year later that the Bitcoin network saw the light of day. The first block was mined. (This was the so-called *genesis block,* which meant the start of the network. The first 50 Bitcoin were created with this block but were completely unspendable!). A secret message was hidden in the block by its creator: "The Times 03/Jan/2009 Chancellor on brink of second bailout for banks." This confirmed the underlying ideas of the technology and the entire cryptocurrency network. Of course, the implementation has been revised by many programmers over the years. Satoshi Nakamoto was only involved with the development until 2011, after which they withdrew from the public scene. It was up to the community to not only uphold the network, but also update it regularly. This meant that consensus was not only something that was used within the algorithm of the network but also by the people surrounding it. As you will find out later, the consensus within the technology proved to be more reliable than the one in the community. Over the years, the Bitcoin network grew (as you without a doubt know to become a huge market). This could not continue unfettered and other competitors joined the market.

In the years that followed, "altcoins," or alternative cryptocurrencies, started to emerge, such as Litecoin, Namecoin, and others. All of these had the same codebase as Bitcoin but tried to add their own twist on how a cryptocurrency should look. Some tried to increase privacy; others tried to increase the amount of cryptocurrencies that were created with each new block, increase the number of transactions, and so on. But the underlying model basically stayed the same. Even though governments all over the world were well aware of the evolution of cryptocurrencies, it wasn't until 2013 that a government took action. The U.S. authorities seized all accounts associated with Mt. Gox, which was a cryptocurrency exchange, because it wasn't registered as a money transmitter. It was the beginning of a lot of misunderstandings concerning the legal context of the blockchain technology and cryptocurrencies. Research would follow, but it would take years before real action was taken to provide a legal framework. To this day, many governments still struggle to create a real framework that can be used by individuals and businesses.

One of the issues that Bitcoin and other altcoins started to struggle with was the connection to drug trafficking and terrorism. As early as 2013, Bitcoins were seized during a drug investigation and, to this day, there are suspicions that some altcoins (certainly those focused on privacy) are used to fund criminal activities. Nowadays, crypto-exchanges need to adhere to the same laws as any other financial institution, including KYC (know your customer) legislation and AML (anti-money laundering) legislation.

Apart from the association with criminal activity, there was another main issue with Bitcoin and similar networks. They used a lot of computing power through interactions across the network. However, developing applications on top of the Bitcoin network proved to be (extremely) difficult. To this day, developers are trying to work out new ways to use computing power to make powerful and trustworthy decentralized applications. One of the developers who was working on a Bitcoin application was a 19-year old programmer named Vitalik Buterin, and he was about to change the world. He saw the potential of the blockchain technology and realized that its potential could go much broader than cryptocurrencies and financial services alone.

It was late 2013 when Vitalik Buterin published his whitepaper ("A Next Generation Smart Contract and Decentralized Application Platform") describing a new way of working and a new open source protocol. The main issue he wanted to solve was that Bitcoin did not have a scripting language to help create decentralized applications. Because it proved too difficult to come to a general consensus within the Bitcoin community, he proposed an entirely new platform: *Ethereum*. It would be officially announced at the North American Bitcoin Conference in Miami, in January 2014. Quite quickly, the founders decided to put the platform and its development in a nonprofit (the Ethereum Foundation). The development would be funded by a crowd sale of the new cryptocurrency called *ether*. The idea of putting smart contracts in the blockchain was specified by Gavin Wood in the Ethereum yellow paper that describes the Ethereum virtual machine.

In July 2014, the Ethereum Foundation held an ether crowd sale that sold over 60 million tokens. About 12 million tokens were created so that the Foundation could fund future development and marketing efforts. A first version of the network was released a year later and was called *frontier*. Any future developments came with new names and releases, proving the evolution that the network made.

Over time, more and more players entered the field with their own implementations of the blockchain technology or distributed ledger platforms focusing on specific target groups (i.e., developers or even business professionals) or industries (i.e., financial services and others). Its popularity increased over the coming years and reached its highest moment around 2018, after which a massive crash followed. In the meantime, around 2015, the Hyperledger project was created, which has arguably incorporated some of the most famous development frameworks for enterprise blockchain today. Over 6,000 altcoins were created and are (more or less) functioning today.

The Cryptocurrency Crash

This section discusses the cryptocurrency crash (also known as the Bitcoin crash or the great crypto crash). A huge sell-off took place in January 2018, leading to a crash in the value of Bitcoin by about 65 percent. A lot of other cryptocurrencies crashed even harder and in some cases completely disappeared from the map. Of course, to have a crash, there first has to be some kind of boom. In the years leading up to 2017, there had been a steady increase in the value of Bitcoin and other cryptocurrencies. In 2017, there was an unprecedented boom in cryptocurrencies and their values. All major institutions and investors seemed to be involved in the cryptocurrency markets, leading to results such as that of Bitcoin, which had grown 2,700 % in value in 2017!

This lead to many small investors being interested in cryptocurrencies, some who also wished to enter the cryptocurrency market and take great risks. This attracted a lot of con artists who wished to take advantage of gullible investors or those who wished to get rich quick, as some others had done in the beginning of the cryptocurrency markets. As there was no clear legal framework, a lot of initial coin offerings (ICOs) were launched, rounding up bigger and smaller investors, which eventually led to abuse and theft of funds.

For those of you who aren't familiar with the term ICO, it is a type of funding where cryptocurrencies are used. These cryptocurrencies can become functional units of currency in case the funding goal is met and eventually the project is successful (which is a big if). To give you an idea, only about half of all ICOs tended to survive longer than four months in the years 2017 and 2018, and still over seven billion USD were raised via ICOs in the first half of 2018 alone! Other schemes involved "pump-and-dump" scenarios, where a couple of people would create transactions between one another, to give the impression of market interest and value. Other investors would invest in the altcoin as well, after which the original participants would start dumping their holdings, leaving the investors with worthless coins.

A final important aspect that one should take into account is that most of the altcoins being launched are grounded in startups. And as anyone knows, startups also tend to fail and with it the cryptocurrency they launched. All of this created a very volatile market in which investors thought they were outsmarting others or could hold out just a bit longer. Even though warnings kept predicting a major bubble, this didn't stop most of these investors.

To give you an idea of the timeline, on December 17, 2017, Bitcoin reached a price of $19,783.06. A couple of days later, on the 22th of December, the price fell below $11,000, which was only one of the many cryptocurrencies dropping to all-time lows. The bad news didn't stop, as rumors regarding possible bans of trading in cryptocurrencies in South Korea led to even more sell-offs. On January 28, 2018, there was a major hack of CoinChck, which was at the time Japan's largest cryptocurrency OTC market (over-the-counter market, where seller and buyer interacts directly), which led to a loss of 530 million USD of NEM (a blockchain development platform written in Java). Other cryptocurrency exchanges were dealing with hacks and irregular trades, leading to even more distrust in the market and investors seeking refuge from the highly volatile cryptocurrency markets. By September 2018, the cryptocurrency market had crashed to less than 80% its original value. This made it officially worse than the dot-com burst that had led to a drop in market value of Internet-related companies from their peak in March 2000, to their low in October 2002, which was about a 78% drop.

Now you know the story, or at least part of it. A story like this one has many different perspectives that one needs to take into account. The most important aspect that I would like you to remember is that none of these issues has anything to do with the blockchain technology itself. Some projects might have failed with certain startups because they were implemented incorrectly. As with any technology and any application, mistakes can be made. Again, this doesn't mean that there is an issue with the underlying technology. Rather, it could be due to people not understanding the technology or how they should implement a blockchain project.

The reasons for the crash were to a large extent financial, as with any bubble, but the scrutiny regarding the blockchain technology has remained. This means that people have become very skeptical about distributed ledgers and, rather than looking into the possibilities of the technology, they declare that they have lost "faith" and wonder why one should "still believe." As I stated, there are reasons to question whether you should implement a blockchain platform, but believing in the underlying concepts shouldn't be one of those.

Now

The cryptocurrency crash has led to major distrust. Since that major crash, other crashes have happened over the last couple of years. Other scandals also have occurred in the field of cryptocurrencies. (The stablecoin Tether is a prime example. Over a four-year period there have been scandals regarding its parity with the USD. There have been problems with audits, independence, allegations of price manipulation, and more. We go in more detail about this issue in the final chapter.) Still, those who really want to do something with blockchain haven't been waiting around and have made taken steps in developing new and exciting implementations. All of this has led to an entire industry of its own, with new developers and architects taking a more prominent position in the new IT landscape. Facebook is trying to launch its own coin with the creation of Libra and other major payment providers are trying to get in the market as well. As Ripple and others are transforming entire industries, blockchain and cryptocurrencies are here to stay, for better or for worse.

The blockchain world has become much larger than we ever predicted, and it keeps on increasing. You have the "classic" open implementations such as Bitcoin and Ethereum. There are currently also "closed" implementations such as Hyperledger Fabric and Hyperledger Sawtooth, which allow you to create consortiums between selected groups of partners that work together. However, don't be surprised if you are confronted with terms such as DAGs (directed acyclic graphs), MerkleDAGs, BlockDAGs, and others. These are all new and exciting ways to implement decentralized networks, and they all want to achieve the same end goals as the blockchain technology. We will provide high-level descriptions later to give you an idea of how these work and in which industry you might adopt or implement a certain platform. For now, we focus on the possibilities of the technology. We will look a bit deeper into the cryptocurrency market as well, but this is certainly not the goal of this book.

Recently we have faced a world crisis, with a pandemic bringing down many a country and forcing us to live in quarantine. This was combined with an economic crisis unparalleled in the history of the world. Many projects were stopped, or at least put on hold, and a lot of people even ended up (temporarily) unemployed. In times like these, people are pushed to the edge, not only to stay safe but also to maintain their standard of living. It is in those same times that people become most creative and some even dare to take risks they normally wouldn't take. I wouldn't be surprised if we see new applications and startups appearing in the coming months (not only in the field of blockchain technology) that will astound the world with their new take on existing problems.

Blockchain Startups and the Future

Before we go into more detail about how the blockchain technology works, let's begin with a short introduction to blockchain startups and the use of the blockchain technology. This will also give you a good indication of how the market value has increased over time. This might give you an indication of the number of implementations that people are working on. One of the other things people just love to say is: "I have never seen a working use case of blockchain outside of cryptocurrencies." Well, let's prove them wrong. Even the most skeptical of people cannot remain blind to the rise in startups that use blockchain technology. While the early startups originated mainly in the financial sector, they have now spread out to cover every possible industry one could imagine. As estimated by the International Data Corporation, the blockchain market has reached a total value of 2.55 billion USD in 2019 and was forecast to reach 55.54 billion USD in 2025. The current economic crisis might have a strong impact on the growth in 2020 and perhaps even in the coming years, but it should still be clear to anyone looking at these numbers that we are dealing with an important growing market that shows promise for the future. Major companies have also implemented blockchain projects in the past, such as SAP, Coca Cola, Alibaba, and many others.

Another important aspect that you need to take into account is the spread of startups and use of blockchain technology all over the world. It is clear that the leading innovations are coming from the U.S. and the East. This should come to no one as a surprise. The U.S. has always been a source of innovation and change, where people dare to take risks. Lots of new startups (also outside the world of blockchain) have seen the light of day in the U.S. and prospered. However, one shouldn't underestimate the influence of China, Japan, South Korea, Singapore, Taiwan, and other countries where technological innovation and the IT sector as a whole has seen unprecedented growth. These countries have seen an increasing level of research, innovation, and risk-taking, which has led to fierce competition with other technology companies across the world.

When we look at the number of startups across the world, we can look at data from Venture Sources-Dow Jones, to provide some information on key world players [A], EU member states [B], and the rest of the world [C] in Figure 1-1.

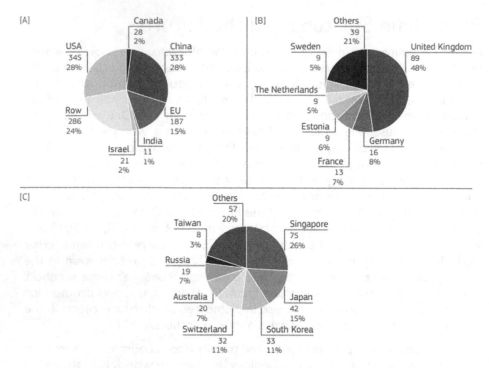

Figure 1-1. Blockchain startups across the world[1]

If we look at this data, the largest number of blockchain startups are in the U.S., followed by China. The EU only houses about 15% of the global startups. This will reduce even further if you see that about 50% of these startups can be found in the UK and Brexit is looming. The EU tries to stimulate further innovation and business creation. The reason for the low number is related to the legal uncertainty when it comes to blockchain technology, the scattered legal landscape, and the difficult decision making at a political level. On top of that, there is a harsher environment when it comes to business risk taking. A business failure in the U.S. is seen as a "good try" and the possible leap to the next, hopefully successful, try, while in many EU member states, business failure is just regarded as a failure.

[1]Figure from Nascimento S. (ed), Pólvora A. (ed), Anderberg A., Andonova E., Bellia M., Calès L., Inamorato dos Santos A., Kounelis I., Nai Fovino I., Petracco Giudici M., Papanagiotou E., Sobolewski M., Rossetti F., Spirito L., *Blockchain Now And Tomorrow: Assessing Multidimensional Impacts of Distributed Ledger Technologies,* EUR 29813 EN, Publications Office of the European Union, Luxembourg, 2019, ISBN 978-92-76-08977-3, doi:10.2760/901029, JRC117255

An important takeaway from the graphs in Figure 1-1 is that most of these startups are flourishing in developed countries, while the possible advantages for developing countries in numerous fields cannot be underestimated. However, the impact of such companies can change dramatically over time, and developing countries could top the list in the near future. The number of new startups that enter the market declined strongly in 2018 (only China saw an increase). It remains to be seen if this signifies a real trend or only a temporary decline. See Figure 1-2.

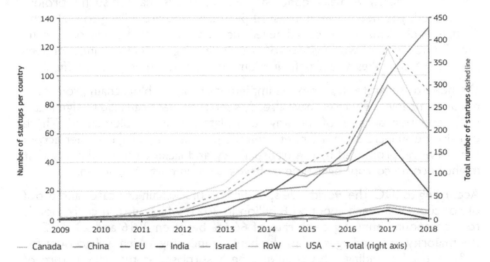

Figure 1-2. Total number of startups. Source: Venture Sources - Dow Jones

The way that most of these startups are funded is using capital funds and ICOs, which shouldn't surprise anyone who knows the industry and the field. The difficulty often lies in making money and a profit after these initial fundraising activities. This has proven to be quite difficult for a lot of these initiatives. Several reasons can be thought of as why there has been limited profitability in pure blockchain markets. One is that it has been difficult for blockchain applications to become mainstream and attract a huge market. Most participants and users of decentralized applications are already familiar with the decentralized world. This is strange as a blockchain application isn't immediately different from any other application from a user's perspective. Market penetration can still happen for some of these, but to this day, this has been very limited.

A second issue that has been plaguing blockchain projects from the very start is scalability. These projects work well to a certain level but, certainly with the more "classic" implementations, the second the number of users started to increase, there was a major increase in the transaction fees or the network started to become congested. Again, new implementations are able to (in part) address these issues and have become much more scalable. Still, these earlier concerns are still following blockchain startups to this day.

A third concern that you should take into account is that projects, more often than not, remain in a kind of pilot phase. Even when these startups provide or create certain platforms and are able to pilot major customers, the customers often don't take the next step. This is because they misunderstand the use of the platform, the way of working, or simply because the change isn't an immediate priority. A major concern linked to this is that for such a project to succeed, you need several invested partners who are willing to make the change. A blockchain project will never succeed if you are the only one trying out the new way of working. So you are depending on multiple independent parties, which makes a successful implementation that much more difficult.

We need to separate this from the implementations of blockchain projects in major companies, where we have already seen that these can lead to significant cost reduction because of the way such platforms are implemented. There can also be an increase in trust between the partners working together across the network, promoted by the transparency and lacking the third party that might become corrupt over time or have a certain cost to maintain.

According to IDC, the worldwide spending on blockchain use cases and proof of concepts will reach about $1.8 billion in 2021, which in turn corresponds to a compound annual growth rate of 66.6% between 2016 and 2021.[2] Still, the majority of spending is led by the banking industry, which will account for 47% of total spending. This shouldn't be a surprise, as the very nature of blockchain technology started in the financial industry (or as a protest against it). They are quickly followed by the distribution and services sector (for 22% of the total amount of investments), where blockchain technology has proven to be great alternative solution to adequately managing supply chain processes. Other sectors that have major investments are manufacturing and resources (19%), infrastructure (6%), and the public sector.

Blockchain has proven to be an interesting and successful tool to help companies transform inefficient processes. The technology itself is an important driver here, but because a new application is being implemented, people and businesses tend to be able to think outside of the box and really change the way they are working. So one can imagine that a blockchain implementation might have a significant effect on any organization. Not only because of the platform itself, but because of the way people dare to think away from classic patterns to new ways of working. This is of course facilitated by the transparency and increased trust the technology facilitates.

---

[2]https://invoicebrokers.com/fr/2019/03/06/blockchain-technology-market-development/

This is why you might imagine that future investments will keep on increasing, as more and more companies will realize the value that can be created by optimizing the current processes they are using. Combine this increased value creation with an open and transparent process in which both customers and legislators trust the way you are working, which leads to even further reduced costs.

Sounds really good, doesn't it? Well, as I said before, there are also good reasons not to implement a blockchain solution. One is that blockchain only works when organizations start to work together. As long as you, your competitors, suppliers, or customers aren't willing to work together, your project is doomed to fail. Blockchain only works when parties are willing to cooperate within the same network and application. Trust can be literally built in within the solutions you are providing. But again, you need the support of every party joining or the eventual implementation is doomed to fail.

Another time that a blockchain platform might not be the best solution for your business is when you are dealing with customized transactions. Customization is something that blockchain applications don't always respond well to. You can of course create your own network, platform, way of working, and decentralized applications. You can also create your own type of order through the use of smart contracts but there must be some kind of common practice for all these orders that can be standardized by using automation. If there is too much variation and change in the type of orders being used, the creation of different types of smart contracts can becomes too much of a hassle and too expensive.

A final consideration is one related to processing speed and scalability. Even though there are platforms and technologies out there that can now carry the burden, only if you make the right choice, you will be able to process them all through a blockchain platform. Otherwise, you might face congestion within the network itself. Depending on the use case, you should take all of this into consideration before making a final decision.

A Quick Technical Introduction to Blockchain

First, I will have to explain in short what public key cryptography is. *Public key cryptography* (or asymmetric cryptography) is generally used to produce two types of keys: a private key and a public key. The public key can be shared with the public while the private key has to remain private (shocking, I know). To generate these keys, a one-way function is used. This came into practice to solve an age-old problem when it comes to secure communication. We all know symmetric key cryptography: you just produce a private key and use it as a password or passphrase for an account, lock, or anything else. Easy, right? Imagine that we want to send messages to one another, which we would like to encrypt so that we are the only people who can read them. We just share the same password, problem solved! Well, not really, because, first of all, we need to find a secure manner to share those keys with each other. This can already pose quite a problem. The second problem is the one of numbers. You might want to send secure messages to me, but I can imagine you would like to do the same with all your friends, family, and colleagues. That are a lot of private keys to send and store! This would mean complete mayhem in the real world. Public key cryptography found the solution here. You can just share your public key with everyone, leave it in a public database, and transmit it over insecure networks. It is meant to be shared and known by everyone. If you now use my public key to encrypt a message, I am the only person that can decrypt it with my private key. See Figure 1-3.

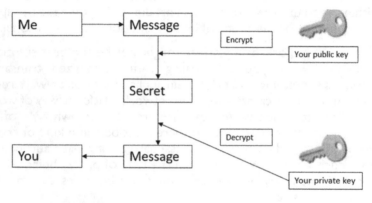

Figure 1-3. Public key cryptography

Some of you might have already made the link to blockchain and cryptocurrencies: your wallet address and the private key you use to access it. Of course, there are many more uses for public key cryptography. Think about digital signatures that are used to verify the sender of a message. The way these keys are generated is more often than not based on hashing algorithms that produce a certain outcome based on entropy. There is a reason why you can no longer access your wallet when you lose your private key. These are meant to be unbreakable. Of course when the algorithm can be broken, your keys can be broken as well. Depending on the blockchain platform you are using, different types of hashing are used to generate these keys. This is also why some coins can be stored together and others cannot. Often there is also some added procedures: this is why the addresses for Ethereum and Bitcoin look so different, for example.

Something else you'll use is *elliptic key cryptography*. This could bring you a bit out of your comfort zone (certainly if cryptography is completely new for you). To start with, we have to talk about finite fields, which can be defined as a finite set of numbers and two operations (addition and multiplication) that satisfy a specific set of rules. The next step is elliptical curves. These are of the form: $y^2 = x^3 + ax + b$. See Figure 1-4.

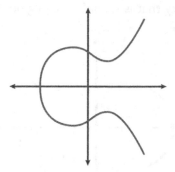

Figure 1-4. Continuous elliptic curve

These elliptical curves are used in cryptography and in blockchain implementations. For Bitcoin, it is $y^2 = x^3 + 7$ or secp256k1 (see Figure 1-5). It is often said that this specific implementation was picked because it has the lowest probability of backdoors being implanted by the NSA. This is why many other blockchain platforms use the same elliptical curve.

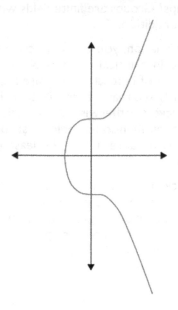

Figure 1-5. secp256k1

But now for the why: why do we need elliptical curves? Elliptical curves are used for something very specific: point addition. Point addition is actually just as it sounds. We add two points that lie on the curve. The weird thing is that the outcome of this addition, a third point, will also be on the curve![3] This is a very interesting property that is thankfully being put to use. See Figure 1-6.

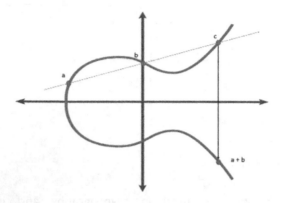

Figure 1-6. Point addition

Now we have come to the end of our journey: we will combine finite fields with elliptical curves. All of this is finally combined to come to the actual core of the business: elliptical curve cryptography, for which we need finite cyclic groups. So what are groups? Groups are finite fields with only one operation, which in this case is point addition.

If you have all of this information, you can start creating your cryptographic curve, which can be used in elliptical curve public key cryptography. It has many uses, but in the world of blockchain it is used for signing and verifying transactions. You can clearly see that it is crucial that these underlying curves cannot be broken by attackers, otherwise the security of the entire system would be at stake. Again, as mentioned before, secp256k1 was chosen by many blockchain platforms because it had the least chance of a backdoor being built in by the NSA.

When we talk about blockchain, we talk about ledgers. In the classic way of working, there is a third-party necessary to verify payments, notarize transactions, use escrow, and allow voting and registration. With the advent of blockchain, we move away from these third parties which centralize power. In itself, centralization isn't necessarily bad, but it often leads to inefficiency,

---

[3]Exceptions are when the intersecting line with the curve is perfectly vertical or when it is the tangent of the curve.

high cost, loss of privacy and control, corruption, and more. With a distributed network, this is no longer possible, as the participants decide the outcome and validity of transactions. There is a single truth that must be supported by the majority, and not by a single power in the network.

People often forget what this technology actually is and instantly start looking at the implementations. However, to understand the possibilities, you first need to truly know and realize what this technology represents. One important part is the existence of a peer-to-peer network. People nowadays are used to a centralized way of working when it comes to the Internet. When we visit a web page, we know that it is running on a server somewhere and that we are visiting the same location. However, this wasn't always the case. The very beginning of the Internet was that of a peer-to-peer network where computers were directly communicating with one another. This technique is still used nowadays to share files over BitTorrent and other networks. A second example is the TOR-network, which is a free, open source network that is used for anonymous communication (it does have a negative reputation, as it is also used for underground activities).

The problem with centralized networks such as the Internet is that there are centralized providers that can provide or deny access, control what is seen, and more. This third party can be hacked, fail, or even become corrupt. This is why blockchain technology moved away from centralized entities in the first place. We remove any centralized servers and allow the participant nodes to directly communicate with each other. Even more importantly are the costs that are brought by third parties. These often make processes overly expensive and make these services cost-prohibitive to a lot of people and (small) businesses. The problem is that these costs are unnecessary for the process to function, as it is only used as a check of compliance. With blockchain, you can automate these checks and reduce these costs significantly.

The final part to understand the technology is the concept of *hashing*. When you hash a certain dataset (this can be a word, a sentence, some numbers, or even an entire book), you receive a unique identifier of that dataset. Whatever the size of the input, the output size will always be the same. On top of that, if you only change one number, letter, or symbol, the resulting hash will look completely different. And when I say completely, I mean *completely*. This way, you have an assurance that the data has not been modified. As you can see in Figure 1-7, the difference between the hashes of the word "apple" and the word "apples" is clear.

Figure I-7. Difference between hashes

There are many different possible hashing algorithms out there, but they need some key features to be successful. One is that they have to be collision resistant, meaning that you cannot find two inputs that will lead to the same output. Another is that they should be pre-image resistant, meaning that you cannot guess the input based on the output hash. These algorithms are commonly used in cybersecurity for password schemes to improve the security of applications. Instead of storing passwords directly, the hashes of passwords are stored so that passwords cannot simply be stolen out of the application (even though commonly used passwords can still be extracted by attackers). In the past, several of these algorithms have been "broken," meaning that one could revert hashes to their original inputs.

How is this applied in blockchain technology? In several ways, as you will see later on. You might imagine several ways that this could be applied in any field. You could take a hash of a document and store it somewhere safe, and if you ever wanted to prove that the document didn't change, you could simply re-create the hash of the document and compare it to the stored hash (this is actually one of the first use cases of blockchain other than cryptocurrency).

In blockchain, this technique is used so that resulting transactions be compared rather quickly. When you start hashing transactions, you can also hash hashes and create from a group of hashes, eventually a single hash. This is called the *Merkle tree* and this can be used to compress a lot of data. The Merkle tree can be used to prove what data is held within a block (see Figure I-8).

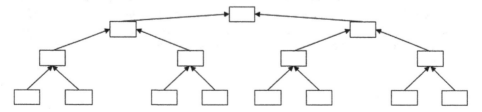

Figure I-8. Simple Merkle tree

All of these blocks consist of sets of transactions that are chained together in one huge ledger. The blockchain, in fact, represents nothing more than a historical overview of the transactions that have taken place in the network. These techniques together help us create an append-only ledger of transactions, which is distributed over all the nodes in the network. These transactions are contained in a linked list of blocks.

Building Blocks

The term "blockchain" refers to the very core of the technology. The underlying data structure is an ordered back-linked list of blocks that consist of transactions. These transactions represent payments between all the participants taking part in the blockchain network. The term "payments" here should be seen as quite broad. It could consist or payments as we know them via cryptocurrencies, but it could also refer to any action confirmation between two parties depending on the blockchain platform. The way the blocks are linked to each other is by using the hash of the previous block that was last added to the chain, as seen in Figure 1-9. If you think about it, the blockchain with the transaction data is nothing more than a ledger where the data has been structured in a different way.

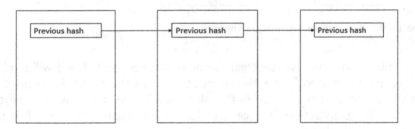

Figure 1-9. Linking blocks together

Because we know that each hash is a unique fingerprint, we can always know for sure that the block is part of the chain. It's important to note here that a parent block (the most recently added block) can have more than one child block, while a child will always have one parent. If there is more than one child, we are dealing with a fork in the system. Normally these forks will be resolved and only one of the children is used to continue the chain (and become a parent themselves). In some cases, however, some of these forks stay on and we will deal with separate chains that all once started from the same parent. We always need to have a starting point, a first block, which is conveniently called the *genesis block*. Because we could visually understand that blocks are being stacked on each other, we refer to the most recent block as the "tip" or "top" and the distance to the genesis block as the "height."[4] The greater this height becomes, the more difficult it will be to change one of these earlier blocks. The longer the chain becomes from a certain block, the more computer power it will require to recalculate the information contained in all the blocks.

What else is stored in the blocks? We have two main parts between which we have to distinguish: the block itself and the block header. The hash of the previous block is one of the items that is stored in the block header. This way, the chain between the blocks is created. That is not the only thing though—depending on the blockchain platform, you can also find the Merkle root, timestamp, and nonce, as well as a couple of other parameters (i.e. difficulty target, version, …). Figure 1-10 shows an example of the Bitcoin blockchain.

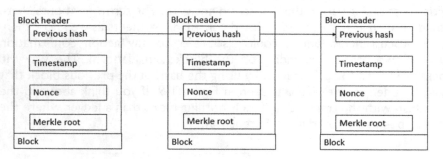

Figure 1-10. Block header information Bitcoin

Not all this information will be clear for now, but no worries, we will explain as we go on in the book. The Merkle root gives us the digital fingerprint of the transactions that are stored in the block itself. This is a "hash of hashes" based on the transaction IDs or "TXIDs." This hash is unique for the transactions in the block itself. See Figure 1-11.

---

[4]One could try to use this height to try to identify a block, but this is error prone, as the height is not a unique identifier. The hash, on the other hand, will give you this unique identifier.

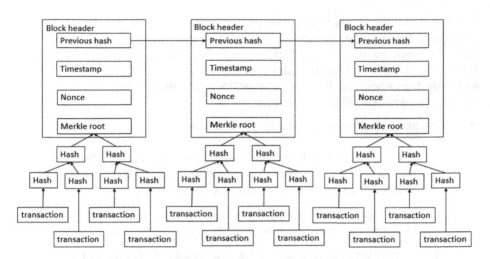

Figure 1-11. What can be found in the Merkle root for Bitcoin

Again, this is a simplified view of what can be found in the block headers. Of course, the block consists of more than the block header. The bulk of a block is made up of the transactions. See Figure 1-12.

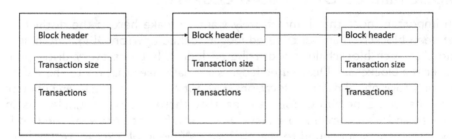

Figure 1-12. The entire chain

As you can see, we are dealing with huge amounts of data, not only in the blocks, but also in the block header. It is the hash that is ultimately calculated from the entire block that can correctly and uniquely identify that block within the entire blockchain.[5] For Bitcoin, the SHA-256 algorithm combined with RIPEMD-160 is used to calculate these hashes, but these algorithms can differ quite a lot depending on the platform you are using. Now that we have an idea of how transactions are put into blocks and how everything is linked together, the main question remains: how do we perform transactions? The idea is that

[5]The hash of the genesis block within the Bitcoin network is 0000000000 19d6689c085ae165831e934ff763ae46a2a6c172b3f1b60a8ce26f

you can sign your transactions with your private key in such a way that it is not only clear that you are the person who is spending it, but also that you have the right to spend it and that you didn't spend the currency twice. Transactions are broadcast through the network and mined into blocks. These will only be processed if these transactions are performed based on the consensus rules that all participants agree on.

In short, the lifecycle of a transaction is as follows:

1. A transaction is created and signed by the creator. This transaction should immediately contain all information necessary to verify and execute the transaction.

2. These proposed transactions are shared with other nodes in the network, which verify them.

3. If accepted, the transactions are propagated throughout the network; otherwise they are discarded. Mining nodes can include these transactions in blocks that can be mined and eventually added to the chain of earlier accepted transactions.

Blockchain or Distributed Ledger?

An important note that I immediately want to make here is the distinction between blockchain and distributed ledger technology (or DLT). Often, it is said that each blockchain is a distributed ledger, but not every distributed ledger is a blockchain. Distributed ledgers are databases that try to share data among geographical different locations without a central actor having control over the entire network. You can see that there are some similarities in concept and what they try to achieve. A major difference between the two is how new data is appended to the platform. While in blockchain technology, one uses a consensus algorithm to add new information, distributed ledgers don't always have such an algorithm in place.

The application of DLTs differs in many forms, as you will see in this book, just as the application of blockchain platforms. The use of the name "blockchain" or "distributed ledger" has many implications. Not only is the technology different but also the perception of the two names. While the first is well-known and hyped all over the world, the second remains more hidden in the shadows and seems to be more known among IT specialists. So why use one name over the other? Some companies want to ride the hype and use "blockchain," while others want to step away from the hype and show that they are really focusing on the technology itself and use "distributed ledger."

Another point you should consider are the "types" of blockchain that currently exist. There are the public, permissionless blockchains (such as Bitcoin and Ethereum), which have no restrictions when it comes to either access or participation. We can also call them the "true" blockchains. We also have private, permissioned blockchains, whereby only a certain group of people can gain access and participate (such as Rubix and Hyperledger platforms). You also have some platforms that exist in between these two extremes. The first are the public but permissioned blockchains that allow everyone to transact and see the transaction log while only a few can participate in the consensus mechanism (such as Ripple and private versions of Ethereum). Finally, there are also the private but permissionless blockchains, where the consensus algorithm is open to everyone while transactions are limited to a specific number of participants. There is no real example available of a network that fully achieves this (the one that comes closest currently might be the Exonum network).

There are also the DAGs, or directed acyclic graphs, which have also entered the blockchain space with their own solutions and networks. To not further complicate the progress in this book, I will treat the term blockchain and distributed ledger as synonyms (I know some of you might not agree with this approach), and I will specifically refer to DAGs when we are discussing them in more detail.

Blockchain Address

The next step in understanding the world of blockchain is the blockchain address. A blockchain address[6] is one of the main concepts within blockchain and cryptocurrencies. It is based on public key cryptography (also known as asymmetric cryptography) where one uses a private key and a public key. As you might infer from the name, public keys are keys that can be known by the public. They are mainly used to identify you, while private keys should always be kept private. They are used to sign transactions or to unlock your cryptocurrencies on your account. There is a wide arrange of algorithms that can create such public and private keys. Over time, because of security concerns, these blockchain addresses have evolved from those public keys to hashes from these public keys. This can be done in a lot of different ways so that for each cryptocurrency there are different blockchain addresses and it is often not possible to send different cryptocurrencies to the same blockchain address (differences in the algorithms prevent this). If payments are being shared over the network to blockchain addresses, these "addresses" can only be unlocked by using appropriate private keys. Based on the manner that these addresses are derived, it can be possible to store altcoins (different cryptocurrencies) on the same address.

---

[6]In the early days of the Bitcoin network, you could pay directly to an IP address. You can imagine several problems with this, such as "man in the middle" attacks. This is why this system was abandoned in favor of more secure options.

Blockchain Wallet

Closely related to addresses is the concept of *blockchain wallets*. These wallets aren't used to store cryptocurrencies, but are used to interact with the network. They are used to generate the information necessary to send and receive cryptocurrency and, to do this, they generate a number of private-public key sets. This can happen at random by using a random seed or this can be based on a passphrase, password, seed words, etc., in something that is called a "deterministic" wallet. The address (as explained before) is used to receive transactions. The private key is used to sign transactions.[7] The wallet software (if we are dealing with a digital wallet), counts the balances associated with each of the addresses in the wallets, creates the sum, and shows this as your balance. So once again, your cryptocurrencies aren't directly stored in the wallet itself. This is rather a more convenient way of dealing with the public-private key infrastructure.

Depending on how you use a wallet, they can be defined as either "cold" or "hot." A *hot wallet* is the easiest to understand, as it is a wallet that is connected to the Internet. There are several providers that allow you to make a wallet. Hot wallets are also called *software wallets* and they come in several different kinds. There are the web wallets that can be created in a browser; another type is the desktop wallet. These can be downloaded on your machine and are therefore considered safer than web wallets. Still, you will have to keep your wallet safe and make backups if possible.

A *cold wallet,* on the other hand, has no connection to the Internet and is used to store cryptocurrencies offline. This is a much safer way of storing (assuming you don't lose your cold wallet), as hot wallets can be prone to cyberattacks. A hardware wallet is a first form of cold wallet. These are physical devices that are used to store tokens for a longer time. There are also implementations that can be used similar to perform transactions. The problem here can be the firmware implementation of the wallet, which is not always as secure as it should be. A smartphone permanently kept offline can be seen as a hardware wallet with similar security. Finally, there are also paper wallets. As you might have imagined, this is simply a piece of paper with QR codes that contain the public and private keys. Paper wallets are very dangerous, as a piece of paper is clearly open to specific dangers. On top of that, these types of wallets can only be used once, to send the entire amount to another address.

Node

When we talk about blockchain and the network it represents, we also speak about nodes. *Nodes* are the lifeblood of the network, as they are always responsible for a given set of tasks. These tasks can include creating, receiving,

---

[7]Or seed phrase, depending on the wallet you are using.

and transmitting a message. Without the nodes, the network would no longer exist, even if the software is still up to date. These nodes are distributed all over the world, across a widespread network.[8]

So what is a node? A node is any electronic device that is connected to the network and has an IP address. One of the main purposes of the network is to maintain a copy of the blockchain and process transactions (depending on the type of node). The owners of these nodes willingly use their hardware, computer power, and energy to maintain the network.

We should also make a distinction between different types of nodes: full nodes, supernodes, miner nodes, and SPV clients. Even though they are equal throughout the network, each type supports the network in a different manner. First of all, there is the full node that downloads a complete copy of the blockchain and checks for any new transactions based on the consensus protocol in use. They are responsible for the verification of transactions and blocks, using the consensus algorithm (explained later). They are also able to relay new transactions or blocks to the blockchain. When this full node is publicly visible, we talk about a *supernode*. The owner of a full node can choose to run it either as a hidden node (not visible to others by using firewalls or the TOR network) or as a visible node. The advantage of a supernode is that it connects to any other node that wants to make a connection and communicates with it, acting as a redistribution point, both for data stored in the node and to facilitate communication with other nodes on the network.

A light node (or SPV node), on the other hand, is referencing the copy of the blockchain on a full node. It is named after the SPV method or "Simplified Payment Verification" method, whereby users can verify if a transaction was included in a block without having to download and maintain the entire blockchain database. These nodes rely on the information provided by supernodes and simply act as communication endpoints (we find this commonly in wallet software).

Finally, we should highlight the difference between a client node and a miner node. While anyone can run a full node (having the necessary hardware requirements), this is not the same as a mining node. When a full node is just validating transactions, we call this a client node. If the owner is willing to invest in expensive hardware (depending on the consensus protocol), he will also be able to mine new blocks while running his node. The concept of mining is explained next.

---

[8]Lisk.io

Mining

Mining is one of the key concepts within the blockchain technology. It is the way new transactions are being accepted within new blocks[9], which are added to the existing chain, as well as how new cryptocurrency is being created. It is always used as a countermeasure against fraud and ensures that all participants within the network remain true. The mining itself is quite costly, as it requires hardware to be used for the mining process, energy to power the mining itself, and time.

Mining takes place in a couple of steps. First of all, the mining nodes need to collect the unconfirmed transactions that are waiting in a pool to be processed. These are forged into a block (which is the collection of the transactions with some extra metadata). Each miner can select the same or a different set of transactions (this can be due to parameters of the node or geographic location). The next step, depending on the consensus algorithm, is to sign the transaction according to the rules of the network. This can be a mathematical puzzle, a number of votes of the participants, or another system. If a valid solution is found, the miner can broadcast his block and solution to the other participants, which can validate the solution. If correct, this is confirmed and added to the blockchain of these nodes, as long as all the transactions inside the block can be executed according to the blockchain history. This is called the *winning* block.

As you saw above, for this, the miner should be rewarded. This is done in two ways: the miner receives the transaction fees of the transactions that are included in the block and the new coins that are being created when a new block is added. The miner can receive this reward based on the algorithm used within the network—proof of work, proof of stake, or otherwise.

The mining process is not only the key to the creation of new cryptocurrency, it is also the mechanism that helps create decentralized consensus in a trustless environment. All nodes over the network receive the blocks and can consequently check its validity. This means that consensus will emerge over time, as there is not an election at a specific time but by an asynchronous interaction of all the nodes in the network. You must realize that in networks such as Bitcoin, the computer power necessary to compete and mine for the next block has increased exponentially over time. This is because of the increase of entrants in the market space and also because of evolutions in hardware solutions. Over time, mining pools saw the light of day. By working together, the pool has a higher chance of finding the next winning block so that the rewards can be shared among the participants. The infrastructure of mining installations has evolved greatly over time and, depending on the

---

[9]In the case of Bitcoin, a new block is added every ten minutes.

blockchain platform, we will go deeper into the when and why of these developments. For some of these platforms, one needs quite advanced infrastructure, while others are still open to everyone.

Of course, when we are dealing with an enterprise implementation of a blockchain platform, you are not going to work with classic miner nodes. Instead you will work with a simpler consensus algorithm in which each participant can easily check and validate what is happening throughout the network. The need for competition is reduced, as these participants actually know each other already so that fraudulent transactions can easily be linked back. This way participants can be removed from the network when they try to cheat their business partners in a consortium.

The Consensus Protocol

We quite often talk about protocols when we talk about blockchain technology. This is of course not something that is limited only to blockchain, but can be found in any implementation of telecommunication technology. When we are talking about a protocol, we are talking about an entire set of rules that decide how you connect to a system and interact with it. These rules can be extensive as they can determine which hardware you have to use, which software is allowed, and what the semantics are of messages that are transmitted over a network. Same as with other telecommunication services. When we talk about open source blockchain implementations, like Bitcoin or Ethereum, there are no restrictions on hardware and the software needed is completely free. Even though this is still the case for private blockchain implementations, one could see future developments where this would no longer be the case.

Proof of Work

Proof of work was the first consensus protocol to be used within a blockchain network. The first network to implement this type of consensus protocol was the Bitcoin network. The idea is that miners have to use their nodes to solve a mathematical problem. It will require a lot of work and computer power to solve, but verifying the result should be easy. This way of consensus is designed to be difficult and to require a lot of fire power. If it becomes too easy to solve, certain security issues could be introduced—mining could become too fast, leading to floating blocks and chains without a main chain. An example is Bitcoin, where the goal is to have a new block every ten minutes. As computing power increases over time, the number of participants increases and the computer power added to the network multiplies. That means the difficulty of the proof of work algorithm needs to become more difficult as well. Some networks have tried to move in a different direction by creating algorithms that are resistant against mining software. Therefore, everyone can keep on mining with classic computers (leaving the network as democratic as possible). A target hash will be set by the network and the nodes have to try to compute a hash based on the block and the nonce that will be below this target number. The lower the target, the more difficult it will be for the participants to find a correct and acceptable hash. The proof of work protocol can help address the issue of Byzantine fault tolerance by using the aforementioned nonce and by combining messages into blocks. To prevent precomputation, the nonce is unique for each node and can only be used once.

An important point of criticism about this type of protocol is the amount of energy that is consumed by networks that apply this type of protocol. In times of climate change, scarce resources, and economic crisis, this is an important point to consider.

There are a lot of different proof of work consensus protocols that are currently in use by several networks.

Proof of Stake

Proof of stake was developed after the proof of work protocol and is more and more being used in blockchain networks. The first network to implement this kind of protocol was Peercoin in 2012. In the proof of stake network, the miner of the next block is selected pseudo-randomly, as the amount of cryptocurrency held by the node influences the chances of being chosen. The probability of being chosen is directly linked to the stake you have in the network.

It is clearly more cost effective than the proof of work consensus protocol, as miners don't have to use energy to solve a mathematical problem. Secondly, it has proven to be more secure. A common example is the 51% attack, where blockchain networks become vulnerable as soon as a participant has 51% of the computing power in a network. From this second, he can validate all his own transactions, against the wishes of the other participants as they can no longer stop him. This might seem contradictory, but the stakeholders with the highest stakes are motivated to maintain the network, because if an attack would occur, this would damage the reputation of the network and hurt these participants the most. There is also a downside to this protocol, called the *nothing at stake* problem. When there is a consensus failure in the network, and the participants in the network have nothing to lose, there is nothing to stop these participants from supporting different sidechains.

Delegated Proof of Stake

The delegated proof of stake protocol maintains an irrefutable agreement on the truth across the network. The protocol uses real-time voting combined with reputation to achieve consensus. This allows every holder of the cryptocurrency to influence the network.

This network uses delegates, which are elected to their roles and have to put a certain amount of cryptocurrency within a base account. The larger this amount is, the more influence the delegate can exert over the network. In case of malicious behavior, the money in this base account is lost. We can also call this deposit-based proof of stake. While the delegates are responsible for transaction validation, it is up to the participants to regularly request if the blocks mined contain all the correct transactions. This ensures that the network is self-governed and policed. You can probably sense that this is more democratic than the other consensus protocols.

Proof of Authority

Proof of authority (PoA) is an alternative that is often used by private blockchain[10] networks (more related to distributed ledger networks), whereby proof of work is replaced by the "identity" of the nodes as a stake in the network. Only the selected nodes are allowed to mine new blocks. These "validator" nodes are allowed to add transactions to the blocks that are consequently added to the blockchain. With proof of authority and validators, there is also the new concept of *reputation*. The reputation of the validators is crucial for the existence of the network. If the reputation of one of the validators or the validator's authority is damaged, the other participants might leave the network or challenge the newly created blocks and its transactions.

This protocol has advantages and disadvantages, when you compare it to the other protocol implementations. The main risk with PoA is that if there is only one validator node, you centralize the risk to a single point of failure. This is a main risk to take into consideration when we talk about distributed networks.

However, PoA does not require the massive computing power that is necessary for networks that use proof of work. PoA also has an advantage over proof of stake. With PoA, the entire identity of a node is put forward. If participants act maliciously, they stand to lose their entire stake in the network. With proof of stake, the participant only stands to lose his current stake that he put forward. This means that someone who has a lower overall participation in the network stands to lose less than someone who has invested heavily in the network.

---

[10]There are also certain public networks that use this protocol.

Other Protocols Used in Blockchain Platforms

Several other types of protocols can be used in blockchain platforms so that one can come to a consensus. One of these protocols, strongly related to proof of stake is *proof of importance*. The difference with proof of stake is that in the PoI environment, the transactions of the user are also taken into account. This way the protocol tries to measure the level of trust and importance of the node in the entire network.[11] Another interesting protocol is the Proof of Activity, related to proof of work and proof of stake. It's more energy efficient than proof of work, as only in the first phase this is used, as in the second the protocol uses a proof of stake. There is also proof of capacity, where the main driver is the hard disk space that is still available (instead of CPU, as we find with the proof of work protocol).[12]

Other protocols that you might encounter are proof of replication, proof of burn, proof of space, proof of space-time, proof of deposit, proof of data possession, and so on. You can clearly see that a lot of different blockchain platforms are experimenting with different solutions to provide consensus in a distributed and decentralized environment and in a secure and efficient way. Each of these protocols has advantages and disadvantages, depending on the goal you are trying to achieve and the way you are working with your organization.

Blockchain Forks

Blockchain forks are an important subject in the world of blockchain. They refer to competing or coexisting sidechains within the same network. Simply because of the decentralized structure of the network, the occurrence of forks seem to be natural. Blocks are propagated through the network and arrive at different nodes at different times. This is can also be the cause of so-called orphan blocks. Normally, the nodes will try to extend the chain with the largest cumulative difficulty.[13]

We can talk about a fork when there are two or more candidate blocks that are competing with one another to form the longest chain. If a miner discovers a "correct" block, it is immediately sent to its neighbors. Several nodes can in time discover a different solution and broadcast this through the network. The nodes closest to the original miners of the block will start building their chain based on this block and continue working on next blocks. If a fork comes into existence this way, the issue is normally resolved within one block. The reason is that one group of miners will find a next solution first, even if the computer's power within the network is evenly distributed among several

---

[11]Used by the NEM blockchain.
[12]It is also called hard drive mining and can be found with the Burstcoin cryptocurrency.
[13]The chain that contains the most proof of work.

competing groups. The next solution will be shared among the network nodes, accepted, and spread through the network. The competing nodes will receive this next solution, accept it, and stop working on the competing solution, thereby resolving the fork.[14] See Figure 1-13.

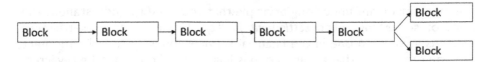

Figure 1-13. Blockchain fork

There is also the occurrence of *hard forks*. This is when there is a software update over the network and protocols or mining procedures are upgraded. Once the upgrade has happened, transactions that are being mined by using the older software will no longer be accepted by the upgraded nodes. This way, a new and persistent branch comes into being. There is a parallel set of transactions that take place on the different chains. A *soft fork* is a change in the software in which only previous blocks and transactions are made invalid while still being backward-compatible going forward. Another difference between a hard and a soft fork is that, with a soft fork, only a majority of the miners need to upgrade. A hard fork, on the other hand, requires all nodes to upgrade to the new version.

Sidechains

With the explanation of forks, you can start to imagine the existence of sidechains. These are blockchains attached to one another (the *parent* and the *child*). Because of this connection, assets are interchangeable over the network at a fixed deterministic exchange rate, while the sidechain can operate completely independently of the parent and use its own consensus protocol. See Figure 1-14.

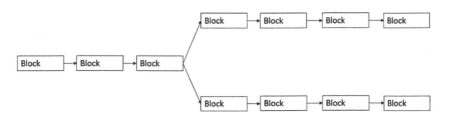

Figure 1-14. Sidechains

---

[14]A fork like this might happen once a week, while a fork that extends to two blocks is extremely rare (because of the explanation in this section).

This transfer is in fact nothing more than an illusion. Tokens are locked in the parent chain and the equivalent amount of tokens is unlocked in the child chain. If you want to transfer, the tokens in the child are locked while the cryptocurrencies in the parent are once again unlocked. For this to be possible, there are several assumptions.

The most important underlying principle that you need to understand is the point of something called *settlement finality*. The concept of settlement finality is a common one in the financial services industry. It is the moment that you can be sure that a transaction is final and will no longer be reverted. In a blockchain environment, where you are working with a proof-of-work algorithm, this moment can be difficult to determine, as at any given point it might be possible (although less likely over time) that a longer chain is created that doesn't include some of the transactions. If we consider public blockchains, using proof of work, a standard is waiting for six confirmations (new mined blocks on top of the block that includes our transaction) before a transaction is seen as final. Its practical implications mean that we have to trust in the honesty of the participants in both chains and that they are both censorship-resistant. All of this requires that the participants are honest, including those participants holding the locked tokens. Otherwise, you enter a situation where locked tokens can be spent and double spending is once again possible.

The child chain can also lack a settlement finality. In this case, one could use so-called *custodians*, which have to vote when to lock or unlock a certain amount of tokens. This voting system can be adapted to any form, which suits the blockchains that are being linked the best. This makes this quite a flexible system to work with. There are several ways that this system can be implemented. The first is by using a central exchange that enforces the two-way peg between the two chains, by only unlocking coins of chain 1 when an equivalent amount of tokens belonging to chain 2 are locked. See Figure 1-15.

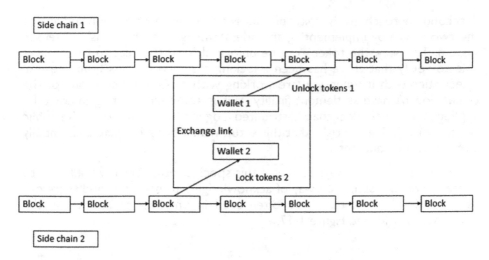

Figure 1-15. Central exchange

You can clearly see that using this system goes against the very nature of blockchain. You are reintroducing a single point of failure and you are once again using centralization. You could try to set up a form of decentralization by using multiple parties that use a multi-signature approach. This is something that could perfectly work in a private setting. See Figure 1-16.

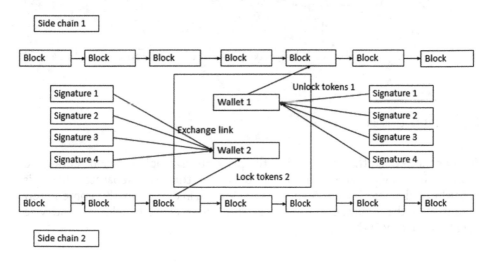

Figure 1-16. Multi-signature approach

A second approach involves stepping away from any centralization and linking the two chains by implementing an understanding of each chains' consensus system. This way, the tokens can be unlocked from the second the chain is able to verify that there has been a locking transaction. This brings several insecurities with it when you are working with a system where one of the chains doesn't have settlement finality. This is something that again could be applied in a private blockchain/distributed ledger setting, but not in the public world, considering the risks that this setup would bring in what is essentially a trustless environment.

You could use several ways to create this specific setup, but it would have to come down to a simplified way of acknowledging transactions and therefore use the Merkle root that is so often used in one way or another in the blockchain world. See Figure 1-17.

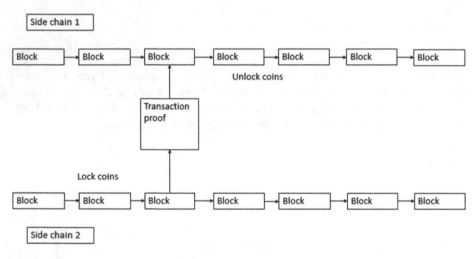

Figure 1-17. Linked by consensus

Another approach that is related to the previous example is called "entangled blockchains." Here, the relationship between the two separate chains is brought to the next level. When coins are locked in one chain, this immediately means that the equivalent amount in the other chain is released and vice versa. See Figure 1-18.

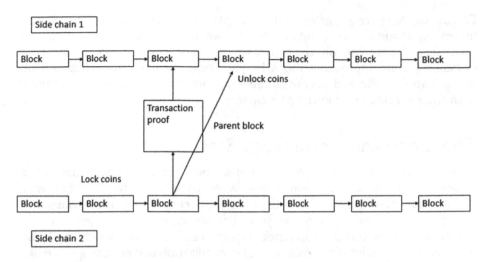

Figure 1-18. Entangled chains

The final example we are going to look at is that of "drivechains." Here, the participants are allowed to vote on when to release the locked coins and when to send these to another chain. These votes can be locked within a certain section of the transaction information. These voters are more often than not linked to one of the chains, determining the actions that take place for the other chain as well. You can clearly see in Figure 1-19 that trust in the participants is the main concern here.

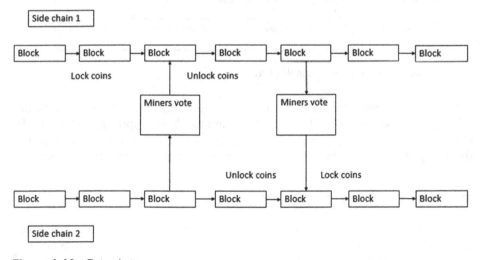

Figure 1-19. Drivechain

Of course, these are all just clear-cut examples that can be used independently. In reality, a number of combinations between these approaches is a real possibility. Depending on the use case you are working on, splitting or combining these approaches might be your best solution. A lot depends on the private—public and permissioned—permissionless approach, combined with the expected trust in the participants.

The Blockchain Technology Stack

Unlike other technology implementations, you have to consider the entire "stack" of the technology when you want to work with it within your organization (see Figure 1-20). At the core are decentralization and consensus. Therefore, you have to look at your infrastructure and ask yourself the question: "are you currently prepared to step in to a new way of working?" You have to, in a sense, let the classic view of centralization and control go to make room for an interconnected system that no longer has a single point of failure.

Layer	Description	Examples
Application	User interface	dAPP, ...
Services	Interconnection of applications	Oracles, wallets, smart contracts, ...
Protocol	Consensus protocol	Algorithms & side chains
Network	Transportation of information	P2P, RPLx, ...
Infrastructure	Node infrastructure	Mining, tokens, nodes, storage, ...

Figure 1-20. The blockchain technology stack

It comes with advantages and challenges, but each of these "layers" has to be taken into consideration when you are thinking about applying blockchain. It is much more than cryptocurrencies alone, as you will soon discover. Keep this image somewhere in the back of your mind as you start your journey.

DAG (Directed Acyclic Graph)

DAGs are another form of distributed ledger technology, just as blockchain is. The main difference lies in the fact that, in the world of DAG, there are no more blocks. This might seem confusing, as you just read that everything in the world of blockchains is basically "chained blocks," but of course, as with everything in life, things just aren't that simple. With DAGs, the transactions are directly linked to each other. Not in a neat little row, more in a cloud of transactions that link to a couple of new transactions and so on. The name itself—Directed Acyclic Graph—actually tells you everything that you need to know. It is *directed*, which means that all links point in the same direction, as you can see in Figure 1-21. Because of this, no loops are possible within the network. It is therefore *acyclic*.

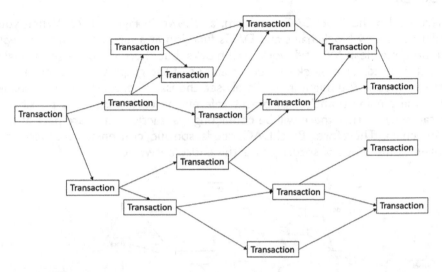

Figure 1-21. DAG at work

DAG basically tries to offer the same functionalities of blockchain but with better performance.[15] It offers better scalability and lower transaction fees (because there are no miners in the network). Contrary to what you have learned from the blockchain technology, here the network will start to work faster as the number of transactions that wait to be validated starts to increase (minimizing the possibility of network congestion). The main concern of DAG at this time is determining the best manner to reach a secure decentralized consensus within the network. When an answer is found to this issue, DAGs might pose a threat to the current blockchain landscape because of the advantages they bring.

DAGs are also often called "blockchain 3.0," as they are seen as the next natural step in the world of decentralized applications and the future way of working. As always, this was just a very broad explanation of what DAGs are. In reality, each implementation differs greatly and comes with its own

---

[15]https://medium.com/nakamo-to/what-is-dag-distributed-ledger-technology-8b182a858e19

advantages and disadvantages. Later on in the section, we will look in more detail at what is currently already there and what will be possible in the near future. There are also MerkleDAGs now, which combine the cryptographic power of Merkle trees with DAG structures.

BlockDAG

There is also the BlockDAG paradigm, as shown in Figure 1-22. When you understand how blockchains and DAGs function at a high level, this concept will be quite clear. We still work with blocks, but there is no longer a single parent. Instead, each block references all tips of the graph that the miner can observe locally. You might immediately see the issue here. As there are many blocks and many branches of blocks referencing each other, the possibility certainly exists that there will be conflicting transactions that are part of the same chain. Therefore, BlockDAG needs specific consensus protocols to achieve some sense of security over the entire network.

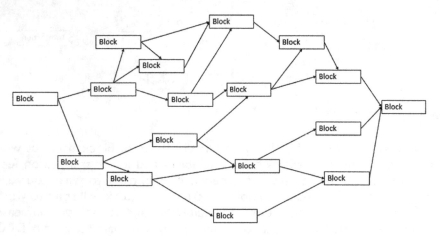

Figure 1-22. BlockDAG structure

With a functioning BlockDAG network, you could speed up transactions to seconds, reduce fees to a minimum, and support network decentralization (because a lot more blocks can be mined). There are fewer orphaned blocks and the incentive for selfish mining is strongly reduced.[16] BlockDAG-based networks try to find a suitable relationship between the networks that were devised by Satoshi Nakamoto, Vitalik Buterin, and DAGs. An example of a network that implements this technology is Soteria.

---

[16]https://blog.daglabs.com/an-introduction-to-the-blockdag-paradigm-50027f44facb

Blockchain and Other Emerging Technologies

Blockchain is not a standalone technology. In fact, it is often used with different technologies. The fact that there are many other emerging technologies doesn't mean you have to choose between blockchain, AI, IoT, or any other type of application; they can enhance each other and create even better use cases for your organization. This chapter describes how you could integrate several technologies to create a better overall solution. Of course, this is only a limited list, as you could pick any set of possible applications and come to a better outcome. You should take into account that this is not always the case, and simply throwing together applications could also easily lead to disaster. When creating a new process or application, or when you want to work with several emerging technologies, you should know that a certain level of risk is involved.

© Stijn Van Hijfte 2020
S. Van Hijfte, *Decoding Blockchain for Business*,
https://doi.org/10.1007/978-1-4842-6137-8_2

New technologies come with unknown risks and every implementation comes with a learning curve. If you are going to combine several of these uncertainties, you introduce even more unknowns. In such projects it is crucial to have oversight and to closely follow up on the developments of the project. Here, we are going to provide some interesting possible synergies and use cases that could help change your organization. We will also provide some examples where these emerging technologies might actually solve current world problems.

Blockchain and IoT

Even though the blockchain technology on its own is very interesting, there are also synergies with other trends that can enhance the blockchain marketplace. While IoT is taking the world by storm with new chips, sensors, and actuators, there are still some major concerns that can be addressed by use the blockchain technology. One of these concerns is the security of IoT implementations.[1] Large-scale deployment of IoT projects has often been hindered by the vulnerability to DDoS attacks. Scalability often proves to be an issue as well, as large networks require a kind of system that allows authentication, authorization, and connection to nodes in a different network, which quickly leads to bottlenecks in centralized network designs. This classic client/server setup leads to an IT architecture that incorporates high costs. That's because the maintenance cost associated with centralized clouds, large server farms, or jusst generally networking equipment, are high. Even though some of these centralized solutions, such as cloud, are sold as low-cost alternatives to a datacenter of your own, these costs can rise significantly. Why? Cloud requires talent of its own, migration efforts, and cloud operations. If not properly managed, this can turn into an infrastructure that's more expensive than the original environment you started with.

Imagine now that you are growing your network of sensors and devices over time. This will only increase the cost and the probably that the infrastructure will not be able to handle the massive amounts of communication that you are sending over the network. This in itself leads to more costs, as information can be lost, slowed down, or deteriorate.[2] Another issue that comes forth from centralized systems is the existence of different cloud platforms between different devices, which leads to even more overhead if you want to control all the data that is being transmitted and shared between the devices in your network. You could of course try to get all the devices on one centralized

---

[1]https://www2.deloitte.com/ch/en/pages/innovation/articles/blockchain-accelerate-iot-adoption.html
[2]https://datafloq.com/read/securing-internet-of-things-iot-with-blockchain/2228

provider, but there looms immediately the risk of vendor lock-in, which is something that companies are experiencing today when they are dealing with their cloud providers.

In the past, blockchain networks dealt with similar issues, certainly when you focus on scalability and security. Blockchain platforms can offer a tamper-proof design, with transparency for the users while still being able to deal with millions and even billions of connected devices and the related incoming transactions. There have been recent platform developments that focus specifically on the IoT industry (i.e., Waltonchain or the IBM ecosystem). Depending on the use case and the future development you want to look into, there are also developments with DAG platforms that are able to deal with high-frequency transaction environments without the network being stressed or clogged up. One of the platforms that uses such a DAG technology is IOTA, with their Tangle.

Another major advantage of the current blockchain platforms is that they are way more cost effective than any of the centralized solutions, as they are able to eliminate a lot of the processing overhead related to traditional IoT gateways. The stability of the network (and the unlikelihood of transactions that have been mined in a block being reversed) leads to an environment in which you can rely on the processed data and analyze it without having to wonder if fraudulent behavior took place during the storage of the data. In combination with smart contracts, this can lead to automated marketplaces, where machine-to-machine transactions become a reality in real-time. You can clearly see that decentralized architectures offer solutions for peer-to-peer messaging designs, distributed file sharing, and autonomous device coordination, all at a lower cost than you would normally have to pay.

However, there are also risks to consider when you look into decentralized architectures based on blockchain platforms. Currently, the blockchain technology is still new, so no organization has all the knowledge in-house needed to develop a complete IT architecture end to end. It therefore has to rely on vendors in the market. These vendors should be looked at with scrutiny. You could face the risk of vendor lock-in, even though the entire idea of blockchain platforms steps away from classic competition models. It doesn't mean that this is the reality. A major risk is the private-public key used in blockchain platforms, where on the one hand, the theft of a private key can enable the thief to sign transactions on the blockchain system. There is, in most cases, no multi-factor authentication yet, leading to a major security vulnerability that hasn't been dealt with. On top of that, the loss of a private key cannot be simply "recovered" and can lead to the loss of funds, data, and the control over the account itself. Imagine building an entire infrastructure to simply lose control over (a part) of it in a second. You wouldn't want a disgruntled employee to have access to such data, as the consequences could be disastrous. There is also the legal and compliance framework, where there is still a lot of uncertainty with the possible legal pitfalls.[3]

Other possible disadvantages are the inability to perform changes to the data. This can be seen as an advantage, when you need to perform modifications, but this almost certainly leads to a hard fork in the network. A final pitfall that you have to consider are the storage requirements. It doesn't matter how you look at it, the storage requirements for the nodes will grow over time. As you are dealing with a decentralized network, this means that several nodes need to replicate the storage of the network. Although you can create networks in which certain data is removed from the nodes, this will grow over time and it is a cost to consider, whether you like it or not.[4]

Despite all the disadvantages listed here, the blockchain technology really can support Internet of Things (IoT) designs to grow in scale for major corporations. By effectively implementing a decentralized platform from the very beginning, this could help companies scale their solutions in a cost-effective way while at the same time considering the security of their network. If you take into account the possible disadvantages and use a risk-based approach, where you carefully consider each step of the design, you could end up being a front-runner in the IoT landscape and reach even more possible customers. You can also focus on further innovation and design. It is up to the bold and the willing to take these risks, but the payoff could be tremendous in the long run.

Blockchain and Artificial Intelligence

Another term that has taken the world by storm is *artificial intelligence* (AI). How you want to interpret AI is up to you, but the link to the blockchain technology is undeniable. While you might not immediately see the connection between the two, as they have completely different developing parties and applications, there certainly are overlaps.[5] So where is the link? Both techniques and underlying technologies focus on the use of data. Where the blockchain technology focuses on the safe encryption of data in a decentralized, immutable ledger, the AI and machine learning industry focuses on the development of engines that enable analytics and decision making based on that same data. When implemented in the correct way, clear synergies can be reached between the two technologies.

---

[3]https://datafloq.com/read/iot-and-blockchain-challenges-and-risks/3797
[4]https://www.binance.vision/blockchain/positives-and-negatives-of-blockchain
[5]https://www.bbvaopenmind.com/en/technology/artificial-intelligence/blockchain-and-ai-a-perfect-match/

The blockchain technology can be used to create data markets, which in turn could be great enablers of the AI industry. They can deliver a sustainable supply of data, which is so vital to this new and growing industry. There have already been some cases in which AI algorithms were integrated within the blockchain platform (an interesting example is Aeternity), or where the outcomes of computation were made available to researchers and the industry to be used in future development. You can also turn this logic around and understand that blockchain platforms can create a clear trace of which decisions were taken by machine learning algorithms and at what moment. If you have a clear set of variables and the decision based on these variables, this can in itself lead to further analysis and optimization of the developed applications.

Other implementations focus for instance on the computing power that is being used for the proof-of-work algorithms. This massive amount of computing power could also be used to train new algorithms and models. It can be seen that several of the companies that focused on blockchain mining farms are now also turning toward the AI industry and offering their computing power for their services. Again, we can turn the logic around and look at the proof-of-work algorithms themselves. While most of them currently have a "brute force" approach, where large amounts of processing power is needed to crack mathematical algorithms, with the use of machine learning, these proof-of-work algorithms could be tackled in a more intelligent way, reducing the processing power needed by these blockchain networks.

You could also use the blockchain technology as the underlying decentralization layer for AI agents that can interact with users. With the decentralized layer, the machine learning algorithms could have a nonstop source of world data without a central entity controlling what data is coming in and how the agents evolve. This could help improve algorithms and how the AI agents respond to the world around them and improve their accuracy. In that same vein, the blockchain technology allows for the encryption of data that is stored on top of it. If you work with sensitive data (think health, personal, or financial data), you could develop applications in such a way that only the machine algorithms could train or respond to the data, without any human participant needing to access it. This allows for a secure layer in which one can store and upload data, to get a response from the AI agent without having to worry about possible security risks underlying their personal data. As mentioned, it could also help create decentralized marketplaces, where individuals are actually rewarded and receive compensation for sharing their personal data. Smaller companies could enter the marketplace without having to compete with bigger tech giants over the data and at the same time prevent big corporations from abusing the data of individuals without them knowing what is happening.

You could also combine the previous story about IoT with AI and the blockchain technology. With all the data coming in from the Internet of Things devices, you can see the value of performing analysis. By incorporating machine learning algorithms in the decentralized platform, you can increase the value from simply using distributed legers to efficiently setting up networks with IoT, by incorporating analysis. One company that already has seen this opportunity is Finalze, which combines wearables with safety regulations in the industry workflow.[6] Other companies are focusing on supply chain optimization, business networks, health data, company energy management, trading forecasting, proof-of-engagement platforms that automatically facilitate payments, capital raising, cybersecurity, and so on.

A final example I would like to share are the efforts being made by Microsoft. The company wants to combine blockchain and AI technology so that people can easily and cost-effectively run advanced machine learning algorithms and at the same time collectively contribute data and improve the models. The blockchain technology allows the creation of a decentralized market, where participants are offered transparency and certainty that they are interacting with the correct code. With smart contracts, participants can receive a payout for the data they provide or the changes they make to the models.

When you consider the previous examples, you can understand that the possibilities are almost endless and the possible outcomes are the same. You should also take into account the possible pitfalls of integrations between AI and blockchain. One is that neural networks need huge amounts of data, for which data lakes are often used. These data lakes (and warehouses) are used to ensure the quality of the data and to make sure that there is always enough data available for new projects and algorithms. A blockchain platform could in part make sure that data quality is respected and maintained. However, as we have said several times before, scalability might prove to be an issue and quickly providing huge datasets might not be that easy with several platforms. This would mean an extra bottleneck and as such actually create a new problem in the world of data markets. This doesn't mean that this has to happen, it only means that one needs to take the limitations of DAGs and distributed ledgers into account when creating an integration that enables data science.

Blockchain and Cloud

As with many other technologies, the big cloud providers also discovered the hype surrounding the blockchain technology and couldn't stay behind. Amazon, Google, Microsoft, and others have all entered the market and provide solutions for enterprises that want to develop a blockchain solution within

---

[6]https://www.finalze.com/

their existing (cloud) architecture. To achieve this, they have set up their own platforms and started partnerships with several startups. An example is the partnership between AWS and Kaleido (which in turn is linked to ConsenSys). In addition, Corda has applications running on top of the AWS cloud platform, and BlockApps can be found in the line of partners.[7] Its aim is to bring the blockchain technology closer to the companies their existing reality and make the entire process a lot smoother.[8] Also, Google Cloud has started partnerships with the startups Digital Asset and BlockApps to increase their efforts on getting an attractive cloud platform for their partners and clients. Chainlink applications can also already be found on the platform[9], just as OneLedger.[10] Microsoft Azure allows easy implementations with Corda, Ethereum, and Hyperledger Fabric technology.[11] Finally, IBM has entered the fray with their own platform and clear Hyperledger Fabric implementations.[12]

I could mention many others here, but the idea isn't to discuss each of these platforms. The main concern is that you should understand the advantages and disadvantages of running a blockchain application on a cloud instance or even "as a service." The advantages of such a setup are clear. As with other cloud applications, it allows you to quickly deploy an application without having to deal with direct infrastructure costs and setup, where you can deploy new machines with the click of a mouse rather than having to install your own machines in your datacenter.

If you combine this with a Hyperledger platform, for example, you can create a consortium blockchain application within minutes that you control. On top of that, you can even more efficiently track ownership if you combine blockchain with cloud computing, as you can develop applications that can replace the current archaic processes, such as clearance through a Depository Trust Company.[13] As with blockchain, cloud computing can help the current trends that further decentralization. This might seem strange at first, as cloud computing is just a different way of using infrastructure (or platforms), but as you know, you can choose different datacenters all over the world to create backups of your data and run applications on remote locations. This can facilitate the creation of nodes that maintain copies of the database and operate independently from each other.

---

[7]https://aws.amazon.com/partners/spotlights/blockchain-partner-spotlight/

[8]https://hackernoon.com/blockchain-and-the-cloud-232c1206a78

[9]https://cloud.google.com/blog/products/data-analytics/building-hybrid-blockchain-cloud-applications-with-ethereum-and-google-cloud

[10]https://www.oneledger.io/blog/oneledger_googlecloudplatform

[11]https://azure.microsoft.com/nl-nl/solutions/blockchain/

[12]https://www.ibm.com/partners/start/blockchain/

[13]https://www.techfunnel.com/information-technology/top-10-benefits-of-blockchain-technology-in-cloud-computing-in-2019/

Here you can also find the idea of edge computing, which has been gaining traction in recent years (certainly with the advent of the Internet of Things). With the blockchain technology, there can be reliable access and control of the network, providing even more possibilities for scaling.[14] With the distribution of the nodes, you can imagine that the geographic risk is reduced (war, natural disasters ...); as there are datacenters all over the world, so that even a private blockchain platform is secured for these types of incidents.

Most cloud providers promise a certain uptime and disaster recovery so that within the sphere of the enterprise, they can secure and maintain a certain efficiency. A next advantage relates to the dwindling costs of cloud computing, which makes it more interesting to use microtransactions. Current developments have shown that cloud implementations can move away from the need to run a full virtual server. Instead, only the operating system has to be replicated to allow the application running, therefore reducing the cost. Finally, there is the idea of distributed supercomputing. Many computers can be linked to a blockchain platform running on top of a cloud-like environment, which in turn can help to partition, manage, and distribute the work over all the nodes. Again, this links to the use of decentralized storage and edge-computation, such as we have seen in the context of the Internet of Things.

You can see that there are many advantages of looking at cloud providers for blockchain applications, but you shouldn't be blind to the possible disadvantages of such an implementation. These disadvantages are closely linked to the disadvantages of cloud computing in general. One is the constant need for an Internet connection to be able to use your services.[15] Even though most major cloud providers have SLAs in place, which promise uptimes of 95% and more, this is something to take into consideration. An argument you could make here is that you also require an Internet connection for blockchain platforms. Well, that isn't entirely true. You could set up a private blockchain network in which you don't need a live Internet connection, or you could use satellite technology or even SMS to communicate transactions. While public platforms generally depend on the Internet, certainly for private implementations you aren't restricted in any way.

A second disadvantage is the use of storage, backup, and computational power in a cloud environment. This differs for each provider, but you shouldn't be blind to the possible downsides. It might seem very affordable now to run a distributed ledger on top of a cloud platform, but as the network and storage grows, are you still able to afford the costs? Is it still profitable to use such an application? In addition, where these questions rise, the risk of vendor lock-in looms in the shadows.

---

[14]https://www.researchgate.net/publication/330592108_Integrated_ Blockchain_and_Edge_Computing_Systems_A_Survey_Some_Research_Issues_ and_Challenges

[15]https://centretechnologies.com/5-cloud-computing-disadvantages/

A third disadvantage is the fact that you are once again trusting a third party (which in itself already runs against the idea of the blockchain technology). You have to be able to trust that this party has a secure environment, reliable datacenters, and a reliable governance framework. If this is not the case, what will you do if something goes wrong? You are simply no longer in control.

A fourth important disadvantage is linked to the third point I made. There has been a rise in the number of hacking incidents with cloud providers. A common mistake is that parties blindly trust their cloud providers to be secure and maintain this security over time. Incidents have shown that this isn't always the case and that there might be incidents leading to data breaches or worse. Once again, you are trusting a third party to provide security to your application.

The world keeps on moving toward cloud-based solutions and infrastructure. As such we shouldn't be surprised that many blockchain platforms have some link to the cloud and uses these infrastructures to help scale the network. The future will clearly see more of these synergies and, when taking into account the possible disadvantages, we might end up with beautiful use cases.

Blockchain and Cybersecurity

Even though there are numerous attack vectors on blockchain networks and technology, this doesn't mean that it doesn't show promise for the future. The technology might even have uses in the cybersecurity world. Currently, it might be one of the best technologies so far to help prevent data theft and fraud. By the very nature of distributed ledgers, one would have to attack and destroy the network to be able to change data and therefore attack the integrity of the data itself. A company that already uses this technology for data protection is Guardtime.[16] Every piece of data is distributed through the network so, when a person tries to alter data, there is an entire system analysis that determines whether the data can be updated or should remain the same. In a similar sense, the availability of data is secured. One can bring down a node of the network, but the data is still provided by the other nodes of the network. An attacker would have to bring down every node on the network to be able to stop the availability of the data. When we are dealing with major networks, this is close to impossible.

Another possibility for the blockchain technology is to create safer DNS services. Currently, these services are centralized and, when an attacker is able to get access to the service, she is able to break the connection between a website and the IP address. With the blockchain technology, one could decentralize part of the service, making it more difficult for attackers to break

---

[16]https://guardtime.com/

the connection.[17] A third possibility lies in the confirmation of identities. With the blockchain technology, one doesn't have to reveal the identity to be trusted. With a validation via a distributed ledger or by using zero-knowledge proofs, one could ensure that the other party can be trusted without revealing any further information about that party. This promotes security and privacy for both parties involved.

These are only a few examples of how blockchain might influence the world of cybersecurity, but you can easily see that more use cases will become available over the coming years. This new technology will prove to be both a challenge and an opportunity to cybersecurity professionals.

Closely linked to the world of security is that of compliance and the use of identity. Both can be enhanced using the blockchain technology. As transparency is promoted through the network, all user actions can be validated and checked so that culprits can easily be identified. Similarly, identity can be locked in and provided by the network, so that there can be no question about who you are and what actions you have taken through time.

Blockchain and RPA

RPA (Robotic Process Automation) is a popular technology in current enterprises. It allows for the automation of standardized tasks and has been marked as one of the disruptive technologies next to blockchain, AI, and IoT.[18] As you have seen in the other examples, there are several ways to integrate these technologies, to come to even greater innovation. One of the similarities between RPA and blockchain is that they both found their first purpose within the financial industry. RPA is seen as a technology that is still in a high growth stage.[19] In the early days, it only focused on simple tasks, but now that more AI and machine algorithms have been added, a smarter way of automation can be provided to many industries.

Blockchain can work as an integrator for an RPA technology, as it can facilitate the processes underlying RPA. This could be done by helping with data exchanges and with deploying agents in a decentralized manner. It could help monitor bots and provide a layer of trust and transaction logs so that you can always verify what the bots have been doing in a secured and reliable manner. If we go one level up, you could also allow network participants to approve the transactions being submitted by the bots. Everything depends on the use case

---

[17]https://www.forbes.com/sites/andrewarnold/2019/01/30/4-promising-use-cases-of-blockchain-in-cybersecurity/#1d7995ef3ac3

[18]https://www.linkedin.com/pulse/integration-rpa-blockchain-potential-new-way-models-parekh-pmp

[19]https://www.gartner.com/en/newsroom/press-releases/2019-06-24-gartner-says-worldwide-robotic-process-automation-sof

and how you wish to handle and automate certain processes. Blockchain could further automate the automation frameworks by providing a decentralized way of deploying bots. Smart contracts can start running when the conditions are met and set off the bots to perform certain tasks. We have timestamped logs, which can provide us all the information we need in case of an audit.

The possible pitfalls include scalability, which really depends on your use case and the platform you are choosing, interoperability with the existing (legacy) systems of an enterprise, and the standardization of the processes you want to implement. Does this mean it is impossible or not advantageous to use blockchain and RPA? Of course not, it merely means that one has to consider each case and map out the implementation in clear steps before doing so, or you'll risk ending up in an endless and expensive project that will not deliver the value it is promising. Other possible constraints are regulatory uncertainty (certainly when we are thinking about personal or sensitive data) and governance restrictions, as companies aren't used to working with decentralized applications.

If everything is properly evaluated, and the project and overall strategy are well thought through, this could help companies expand their efforts and increase the value they are gaining from RPA projects. They can allow bots to span multiple departments and interact with many different users while still maintaining control.

An interesting use case for the combination of RPA and the blockchain technology is that of hospitality programs.[20] By handling user requests, sales, and actions in an automated way, the underlying ledger could be used to log and reward loyalty points and transactions. It could also be used in compliance management, resource management, and supply chain solutions that incorporate RPA bots.

Blockchain and Quantum Computing

When developers talk about the blockchain technology, discussions on the possible impact of quantum computing in the near future will quickly arise. If this is the first time you've hear about this, welcome to the party! Why are there discussions when we think about blockchain and quantum computing? Well, in short, quantum computing might be able to break the encryption algorithms that are currently used in most blockchain implementations, therefore effectively breaking the security they are supposed to bring. Most of the computational algorithms and data structures that are in use today are meant only for classical computers and don't take the advent of quantum

---

[20]https://www.hospitalityupgrade.com/_magazine/MagazineArticles/The-Potential-for-RPA-and-Blockchain-to-Transform-Hospitality.asp/

computing into consideration.[21] Most of these algorithms have equivalents in the quantum computing world, but could have much greater processing powers than is currently the case.

Where classic computers use ones and zeros, quantum computers introduce a third state, called the *superposition,* where a one and a zero can be represented at the same time. So where you would normally choose either a one or a zero and analyze the case sequentially, with superposition you can represent several cases at the same time and speed up the analysis. Because of this, quantum computers will be able to solve problems and break algorithms which don't seem possible. Some of these algorithms would require billions of years to solve classically, while quantum computers could significantly reduce the time needed to do so. While the inside of a quantum computer needs to remain sufficiently cool, the electricity use would also be reduced significantly when compared to classic computers.

While research on quantum computers spans already a couple of decades, some of the first real implementations have started to become a reality over the last couple of years. This is why it certainly deserves attention today, so that we might prepare ourselves for the near future. By speeding up this otherwise "slow" algorithms, quantum computing can cause the destruction or break down of specific information systems. In the case of the blockchain technology, there are two specific threats to the current platforms.

The first is the possible attack on the hashing algorithms used. The underlying assumption of using hashes is that reversing these are computationally expensive and difficult to perform. If quantum computing can easily break these hashes, the entire security that is introduced by the blockchain technology is moot. The authenticity of upstream blockchain and the authenticity of entries are both compromised. This would mean that attackers could modify data in the blockchain without actually changing the hash (hash collision). A second possible issue relates to the mining of new blocks, certainly when a proof-of-work algorithm is being used. A miner with a quantum computer can calculate the nonces faster, outperforming the other miners in the network, therefore not only earning more cryptocurrency than the other miners but also taking control over the new block generation as a whole. Attacks on the public-private key patterns that are commonly used within blockchain platforms are susceptible to attacks by quantum computers. This way attackers could possibly forge signatures, messages, and more, breaking down once again the security of the blockchain network. One can easily understand that the impact of quantum computers will stretch much further than only blockchain networks. In the past this was mainly seen as a

---

[21]https://www.researchgate.net/profile/Brandon_Rodenburg/publication/ 322132176_Blockchain_and_Quantum_Computing/links/5a46b9a00f7e 9ba868aa5375/Blockchain-and-Quantum-Computing.pdf

theoretical discussion that might have an impact in the future, but recently Google has claimed that it reached quantum supremacy.[22] Although that doesn't mean that we will have full-fledged quantum computers on the market any time soon, it does mean that other parties will reach this state as well and develop it further over the coming years. This in itself should be alarming enough for any participant in looking into how we might secure blockchain platforms (and encryption algorithms as a whole) in the near future.

Now that you've learned a bit about how quantum computing might impact the blockchain technology, there is also research being done on post-quantum cryptography. There is currently a process in place at NIST (National Institute of Standards and Technology) to research some options for the future, but currently there is no standard in place. Some of the promising areas so far are the following[23]:

- *Hash-based cryptography.* The classic example is Merkle's hash-tree public-key signature system (1979), building on a one-message-signature idea of Lamport and Diffie.

- There was the design of the Supersingular Isogeny Diffie-Hellman (SIDH) by David Jao and Luca De Feo.[24]

- *Code-based cryptography.* The classic example is McEliece's hidden Goppa-code public-key encryption system (1978).

- *Lattice-based cryptography.* The example that has perhaps attracted the most interest, but not the first example historically, is the Hoffstein–Pipher–Silverman NTRU public-key-encryption system (1998).

- *Multivariate-quadratic-equations cryptography.* One of many interesting examples is Patarin's Hidden Field Equations (minus variant) public-key-signature system (1996), generalizing a proposal by Matsumoto and Imai.

Of course, these examples emphasize the use of traditional algorithms in a new way, while new algorithms might also build on top of quantum technology features. One of these possibilities might be Quantum Key Distribution (QKD), which is a protocol that can generate a random bit stream between parties. This can be used as a one-time pad or Vernam-cypher for further

---

[22]https://www.newscientist.com/article/2217835-google-has-reached-quantum-supremacy-heres-what-it-should-do-next/

[23]https://www.researchgate.net/profile/Brandon_Rodenburg/publication/322132176_Blockchain_and_Quantum_Computing/links/5a46b9a00f7e9ba868aa5375/Blockchain-and-Quantum-Computing.pdf

[24]https://www.esat.kuleuven.be/cosic/elliptic-curves-are-quantum-dead-long-live-elliptic-curves/

encryption purposes. (A *one-time pad* is an encryption technique that currently cannot be cracked or broken. With the introduction of quantum technology features, we might introduce even higher security.) So far this is the most mature technology in the field and as such a very interesting one to look at for near future implementations in blockchain networks. On top of this algorithm, one could also use a quantum system so that the information in the blockchain is tamper-proof. Finally, there are also quantum bit commitment protocols that could replace the current digital signature schemes.

As you can see, the advent of quantum computing will not necessarily mean the death of the blockchain technology. It means that the technology will have to adapt to the rise of quantum but ample research is being done in this field.[25] The impact of quantum will be much broader than the blockchain space alone, and it will be more than interesting to see how the technologies underlying blockchain platforms transform in the future.

Blockchain and Smart Cities

The idea of the smart city isn't a new one. For those of you who aren't familiar with the concept, *smart cities* use modern and smart technology to deal with many issues related to the smooth functioning of a city. As people are moving more to cities, we are faced with increasing traffic, health issues, climate change, scarcity of commodities, population growth, the rising number of elderly, access to education, rising poverty, and so on. The key to this story is the use of the Internet of Things, as these can help us deal with these issues in a modern way.

A perfect example is Barcelona, which saved up to 75 million Euro of city funds and created over 47,000 jobs in smart technology by running fiber optics throughout the city. Street lights use LEDs, which are not only energy efficient but also reduce produced heat. At the same time, they have been fit with sensors to gather information about pollution, noise, humidity, temperature, and the presence of people. A second example in Barcelona is the use of smart bins, which use a vacuum and store the waste underground to reduce the smell of trash. There have also been sensor implementations all over the city so that noise can be managed better in areas with lots of tourists and the city gardens receive just enough water. Finally, the city has several "labs" where its citizens can help develop new digital innovations to make the city even smarter! Other cities all over the world are quickly following. We cannot underestimate the issues we are currently facing and have to deal with them as soon and efficiently as possible.[26]

---

[25]https://arxiv.org/pdf/1705.09258.pdf
[26]https://www.forbes.com/sites/chrissamcfarlane/2019/10/18/are-smart-cities-the-pathway-to-blockchain-and-cryptocurrency-adoption/#386447764609

Blockchain and cryptocurrencies can also play an important role here. All over the world there are POCs taking place, some more successful than others. If we look at some of the major implementations, we have seen that India has several implementations for its major cities to help with transaction management, Dubai is planning to be the first blockchain-powered smart city by 2021, and Estonia has been tracking its citizens with the technology since 2012. (Before you start feeling alarmed, Estonia tracks the data of its citizens to protect them. Examples are preventing the possible abuse of personal and health data or preventing the manipulation of defense data in times of war.) In the Chinese city of Yinchuan, inhabitants can pay for their purchases by using facial recognition and the blockchain technology, taking away the need to pay with physical money. If we look at the U.S., we have places like New York and Virginia that have set up environments to trade electricity and vote via mobile phone.

It can help with decentralizing city management over all concerned partners, linking all of the concerned stakeholders together and pooling their resources.[27] Another major advantage is the introduction of broader participation, which in itself increases democracy when it comes to city management? It can help link the citizens to their cities and gain trust once again in political and administrative institutions (where this is currently dwindling in many places). It also increases the transparency of the decisions and shows how these decisions are handled. Other advantages of the technology are once again the secure management of IoT devices and the control that citizens can have over their own personal data and identities. In line with this, the blockchain technology can help manage privacy in an efficient manner.[28]

Of course, such technologies could also be used for nefarious purposes too. They help control major urbanized areas, and therefore they could introduce the "big brother" idea that we all fear. In the wrong hands, any technology can be misused, but imagine a blockchain-powered smart city where the government controls your identity, movements, and data. It would effectively become a prison for anyone living within its bounds.

Several platforms specifically focus on the development of smart cities. There is the United for Smart Sustainable Cities (U4SSC) from the UN, which wants to drive information and communication technologies for smart and sustainable cities. FIWARE is an EU project that offers a free software platform, and it does not solely focus on smart cities but certainly can offer services that might ease the development of smart cities. DownTown is a third example and it already has 13,000 to 20,000 domains in smart cities around the world.

---

[27]https://www.ie.edu/insights/articles/blockchain-the-decentralized-government-of-smart-cities/

[28]https://www.iberdrola.com/innovation/blockchain-for-smart-cities-urban-management

Blockchain and the Environment

Anyone following the news cannot deny that climate change is a hot topic right now. Not moving into the discussion of climate change itself, the blockchain technology can help protect the environment in several ways.[29]

The blockchain technology could facilitate carbon emission trading, not only allowing for smooth transactions but also providing transparency and security to all participants. This could open up the market even further and give insight into the processes taking place in such markets. There have also been proof-of-concepts in clean energy trading. On such platforms, consumers could buy and sell renewable energy. As blockchain has a clear background in finance applications, this could also facilitate transparent and traceable financing for climate change organizations and initiatives. Risky investments can be optimized with the use of smart contracts and automatic handling of money, taking out the human factor.[30]

Similarly, the use of blockchain allows for the tracking of supplies. This can help further the protection of the environment. Blood diamonds can be stopped and the supply of animals and meat can be thoroughly checked via smart contracts and IDs. This could help promote an ethical and ecological supply chain, whereby businesses using a different route could be held accountable for their actions.

A third example is the protection of endangered species by using tags and tracking data, so that the data security can be ensured by only allowing specific people access. This data can also be used for biological studies. Another way of looking at it is to share data about animal trafficking all over the world so that a clear view can be created about the illegal supply chain. This means the big players can be identified and consequently stopped.

Once again, we shouldn't be blind to the disadvantages that the blockchain technology has brought in terms of the environment. Several reports have warned that the energy consumed by the Bitcoin network alone could power a small country.[31] It is not difficult to see (even when there are certain people claiming that most of the network is running on renewable energy)[32] that this is devastating in terms of climate change. One way of dealing with this massive computer power and energy consumption is by moving to different ways of mining. This has already been done (or is on its way) on several other networks, reducing the computing power needed and hence reducing the energy consumption by these networks.

---

[29]https://unfccc.int/news/how-blockchain-technology-could-boost-climate-action

[30]https://sustainablebrands.com/read/finance-investment/blockchain-and-the-climate-crisis-beyond-the-hype

[31]https://www.nature.com/articles/s41558-018-0321-8

[32]https://www.vox.com/2019/6/18/18642645/bitcoin-energy-price-renewable-china

Blockchain and Poverty

The blockchain technology could also prove to be a weapon in another of the world's major problems: poverty. Two-thirds of the world population lives on less than $10 a day and every tenth person lives on less than $1.90 per day.[33] Many nonprofits try to help and receive financing from people and governments. Blockchain could help track where all this money is going. Donators often wonder what happens to their money and with a distributed platform this no longer should be a problem. Nonprofits could provide clear and immutable logs so that donors could see what happened to their money. In a similar sense, we could trace the results of the work performed by the nonprofit. Donors would have a direct view of what is happening and might become even more motivated to share part of their wealth.

As always, there is also the use of the blockchain technology as a cryptocurrency where transactions could be directly performed between peers. This could, on the one hand, help with donations, but more importantly could support financial inclusion. Many poor don't have access to financial services, which is actively locking them out from major parts of life. With access to decentralized financial services, another issue arises naturally: identity. As this can all be created with decentralized technology, the poor could finally partake in all activities in life without limitation. As people would gain the right to enter formal businesses, pay debts, buy rights of properties, verify ownership, transfer ownership, perform payments, and more, the poor wouldn't be automatically locked out of society by default. In a similar manner, nonprofits could use solutions that could help prove identity and verify certifications from people all over the world.

Is blockchain the wonder technology that will finally eradicate poverty and solve all the world's major problems? No, of course not. But we cannot deny the fact that there is certainly potential. Distributed ledgers could prove to be the extra push the world needs to create an equal playing field for all people.

Limitations of the Blockchain Technology

While a major part of this book is focused on the advances brought by the blockchain technology, we still have to keep in mind that all technologies have their limitations. It is important that you understand when to actually advocate for the implementation of a blockchain-based solution and when situations call for other solutions.

First of all, there are limitations that are core to the blockchain technology itself. There are the limitations brought by scalability issues that are often part of such distributed networks. While proof of concepts might be working

---

[33]https://ourworldindata.org/extreme-poverty

great, the question always remains if the same use case rolled out in a major organization can still function properly. Certainly public blockchain networks are plagued by issues when it comes to scaling and the costs that come with it. If a use case becomes too popular, the entire network can start to slow down significantly, bringing problems to all the other decentralized applications running on the platform. Liveness is another part that can often lead to issues, just as block size, block time, transaction propagation through the network, privacy of transactions and or participants, and security specific vulnerabilities are. These specific vulnerabilities lead to solutions, such as offline hardware stores that cryptocurrencies to prevent theft. Others focus on scalability by creating alternative layers on top of blockchain networks, solutions that have to bring interoperability between such networks, alternative protocol implementations, and more. This brings with it the need for technical expertise of developers and IT architects to know lots of separate solutions and platforms— including their advantages and disadvantages.

When one chooses to develop decentralized applications, this can also lead to several difficulties. If you want to update a DApp, you have to propagate that update through the network and the nodes still have to choose if they accept the update or not. This way, security vulnerabilities could remain within the application in those nodes that refuse the update. Similarly, if you want to update the network, this could lead to a hard fork that brings with it possible divisions in the network.

Beyond the obvious fact that technical knowledge is a key factor in deciding to use blockchain solutions, you must also consider the business model that is being implemented. Oftentimes, this is not in line with the advantages that are brought by the blockchain technology. Distributed ledgers bring with them an entire philosophy of decentralization and moving away from the classic solutions that promote business centralization. Working together and bringing the customer central in the value chain and experience are the key concepts that lead this change. If you are unwilling to implement these changes in your current business, it is often questionable if you will gain any real value from implementing a decentralized application or blockchain in your current IT architecture and operations.

We have also introduced many positive use cases where the blockchain technology can change the world in a positive way. However, we shouldn't remain blind to the fact how it could be used in a negative way (just as all other technology implementations). There have been reports where cryptocurrencies have been used to fund criminal activities, commit fraud, and launder money. Where we propose solutions to help the world, governments wanting to impose control over its citizens might use it in a similar fashion. It is up to us to remain vigilant and support the move toward positive solutions.

Blockchain and Industry Use Cases

This chapter introduces some interesting use cases in a myriad of different industries. For some of you, the reason might be obvious. When you start a discussion about the blockchain technology, many people like to say that they still haven't seen a working implementation in an industry, except for cryptocurrencies. Well, here we leave the theoretical path and show cases that are actually in use today. While there is still work to be done on the blockchain technology, this hasn't stopped industry leaders from implementing the technology and changing the way they work.

Blockchain and Finance

With its very nature set in finance, blockchain technology can offer various solutions in the world of finance to improve existing markets or help create entirely new ones, depending on the use case and the creativity of those willing to investigate the opportunities. However you look at it, distributed data storages can help facilitate how data is provided in real-time to all parties that wish to participate in the market. This way there can no longer be a

S. Van Hijfte, *Decoding Blockchain for Business*,
https://doi.org/10.1007/978-1-4842-6137-8_3

discussion about who has access to market data in a fair manner. Marketplaces could be created where assets are traded over the blockchain platform, just as crowdfunding solutions that allow for smaller projects and companies to find funding. Assets can be transferred in a way that is transparent to all participants, easily verifiable, and cost-effective. Clearing and settlement processes can be fully automated and logged when using smart contracts.

For the regulators, trade surveillance should no longer prove to be an issue, with clear and immutable logs of each transaction. Money transfers can happen without the interference of third parties that claim their share of the transaction. Interbank payments could happen smoothly without time being lost and data could once again be shared with interoperable systems. Financial inclusions could be achieved for those that have no access to financial services and are left in the cold by the current institutions. By allowing these individuals to partake in these processes, we could provide them with better lives and ways of living. Foreign exchange, just as any other form of payment system, could happen over distributed ledgers, improving the current legacy systems that are in place and again eliminating the third parties that take their share.

Entire loan markets could be facilitated over blockchain platforms. People who currently have no access to loans and are left to the sharks that profit from their misery could find a sustainable solution by using microloans or new types of contracts that are built to their needs. The letter of credit is also a classic bank product for business partners all over the world to work and trade with each other. Again, blockchain technology could help to optimize and automate existing processes and reduce costs. There have also been talks, startups, and applications that focus on the creation of derivatives, margin calls, CDS, swaps, and stocks. The possibilities are endless, depending on how you look at current processes or what you can imagine for new products.

The Finance Department

It might be interesting to take a look at the finance department and spot the opportunities within the confines of this department. As always, every project impacts other departments and the company as a whole. However, you can easily see that when you start projects within that same finance department, you can use them as a center of innovation, which in turn can change the entire organization. By the very nature of the technology, this could even include the supply chain, the suppliers, and the customers.

ERP

So, why would you consider integrating your ERP system with blockchain technology? This might result in several advantages. As the Enterprise Resource Planning system is used to manage accounting, procurement, project management, and supply chain, data accuracy is of key importance. It is used to centralize all business data, which allows deeper control over the business operations and the decision making. However, data accuracy cannot be assured, human errors can be made when creating bookings, and the master data might be wrong, all which lead to mistakes in reporting, payments, and so on.[1]

The blockchain, which offers an immutable ledger and promotes transparency, can be an interesting option when you think about data and ERP systems. It could improve auditability as well, as all transactions are locked in a blockchain so that no changes can be made at a later point in time. This naturally also increases the security of the data being stored on the ERP, but on top of that, the mechanism of private keys ensures that only certain people can access the system. Smart contracts could add extra functionalities and automate intercompany transfers, order handling, procurement requests, and payments. This in turn could speed up the processes that are currently often done manually or by partial automation. All of this could lead to reduced costs due to both process optimization and the reduction of intermediaries in the process.

One supporter of such integration between ERP and blockchain is SAP.[2] SAP seems to have several ideas when it comes to the blockchain technology and their ERP system. One of those is manufacturers, as various types of information can be logged and shared within the same ledger. By giving access to major stakeholders, specifications about machinery and product manufacturing can be retraced. With SAP Leonardo, SAP cloud platform, and SAP HANA, the possibility to use Hyperledger Fabric or multichain allows for blockchain integration within current ERP environments.[3] Another initiative of SAP focuses on the pharmaceutical supply chain, where the "SAP information collaboration hub for life sciences" is used in the battle against counterfeit drugs. Other examples where SAP is exploring such possibilities are tires, tech, and shipping.

Another company that has explored the possibilities is IBM, with its Oracle Enterprise applications team, which works on solutions that integrate blockchain with the Oracle ERP cloud.[4] They see opportunities for manufacturers (details for each component of a product shared among the stakeholders), finance (transactional data from multiple financial systems can be collected in one environment, which eases the audit trail and compliance to company policies), law (shared repositories of legal documents), and food services (real-time follow-up on the food supply chain).

---

[1]https://medium.com/@eoscostarica/why-integrating-erp-systems-into-blockchain-is-a-great-idea-e384b298a4a8
[2]https://blogs.sap.com/2018/03/20/how-erp-is-incorporating-blockchain-technology/
[3]www.sap-press.com/introducing-blockchain-with-sap-leonardo_4843/
[4]www.ibm.com/blogs/insights-on-business/oracle-consulting/reinvent-erp-processes-blockchain/

CRM

CRM (Customer Relationship Management) systems are used to improve the customer relationship of enterprises. Even though not directly related to the finance department, they allow companies to increase customer retention and follow up on opportunities. On top of that, it also allows for automation of certain tasks, closer control over processes, and the clear value of statistics and reporting, which allows for improvement opportunities within the enterprise.

Salesforce understood the possibilities of the blockchain technology and integrated it in their Customer 360 platform.[5] They offer the blockchain technology to capture activities that have taken place on the platform and deliver this data to specific workflows, which allow for automation and standardization. When data can be provided in such a fashion, it allows for data analysis, uses data for chatbots, and of course creates an audit trail. The underlying distributed ledger technology can also provide the data to other applications and apps or even to other partners in the business network of the enterprise.

Other Systems

As the blockchain technology becomes a feature in more and more CRM and ERP systems, it can be integrated with other financial and asset management systems without the enterprise having to worry about major changes when one of the applications releases a new update.[6] Once it's integrated, it will have a major impact on how companies are currently working. Processes and workflows can be further automated, data can be standardized and shared among applications as well as with all partners in the business network. This in turn will lead to better business relationships, as necessary data can be shared and changes will be clearly exposed with audit trails.

These data stores can in that sense also be used for new projects, such as better forecasting of sales and the supply chain, increasing the compliance of the overall process, improving the accounts payable and accounts receivable processes, and reducing costs.

Invoicing

Another major aspect is dealing with invoices. Many solutions attempt to deal with accounts payable and accounts receivable. Several blockchain startups have created solutions for existing problems in this area. Distributed Ledger

---

[5]www.salesforce.com/products/platform/products/blockchain/
[6]www.computerworld.com/article/3438838/gartner-blockchain-will-be-noth-ing-more-than-an-add-on-for-erp-crm-software.html

Invoice systems that focus on invoice discounting have entered the marketplace to create more efficiency.[7]

One solution is Populous World, which focuses on invoice financing.[8] With invoice financing, cash that is locked up in outstanding sales invoices is unlocked because buyers can buy the invoices at a discounted rate. Both invoice factoring and invoice discounting are offered on top of their platform, where they claim to be able to open up finances much faster than other partners, while companies retain up to 95% of their invoice value. One of the key items they like to show is that there are no fees for invoice buying, there are high returns, and the market becomes more globalized. With the use of blockchain, they open the market on a global scale while at the same time introducing transparency and security. Also, third parties and financial institutions are removed from the process in the finance system.

A second example is Prontapay, which aims at using smart contracts to help businesses more efficiently get paid with lower transaction fees while using a stable, fast, and secure invoicing system.[9] Because invoices are sent over a blockchain platform, the smart contracts make sure that the "legal coding" creates a binding agreement between the buyer and seller.

When you take the previous example, you can easily see that the data used to create the legal contract code can be used to feed it directly to ERP-systems so that the entire invoice cycle can be automated while keeping a clear audit trail.

Data Dashboarding

One final example is the Anaplan platform (but one could easily say the same for other dashboard or planning software). Blockchain technology can provide data in a similar way as Anaplan takes data from accounting systems today. Distributed ledgers can provide more data if it is in a shared environment, in a standard format, and includes a clear change log. This allows forecasting to become even more streamlined and compliant with the new regulatory reforms established by IFRS and other solvency frameworks.[10]

Qlik has started to look into how data linked to the blockchain technology can be visualized in an effective manner. Whether it's the connections between pieces of data, time series data, or data at scale, Qlik can offer a solution so that you can create deeper insights into your blockchain networks.

---

[7]www.frontiersin.org/articles/10.3389/fbloc.2019.00013/full
[8]https://populous.world/
[9]www.kickico.com/hi/campaigns/59764/prontapay-invoice-solutions-for-the-blockchain-era
[10]www.anaplan.com/blog/analyzing-planning-blockchain-data/

The process of checking data quality and data transformations can be largely automated. By creating a trusted data store with a clear compliance network surrounding it, the lives of data scientists, reporting professionals, and regulatory experts can be easier, and further investigations become possible. This can allow for further optimization of the organization as a whole.

Assurance and Auditing

A classic part of the business process is the audit and assurance process. They are key in making sure that reports have a foundation in reality. If there are certain assumptions made, the auditors have to make sure that they hold up. They have to ask questions relating to missing funds or inconsistencies, and so on. With the distributed ledger as an immutable representation of data, this could have a clear impact on how audits are being performed. Transactions that have taken place can easily be verified on such ledgers without a shadow of a doubt.[11] As in all the other industry scopes we have seen so far, you should understand that there is a major opportunity for automation. The existence, accuracy, and completeness of information can all be locked in the ledger and be checked with smart contracts.

Of course, as we have already stated several times, one shouldn't trust blockchain technology blindly. As with any new technology, there are possibilities for fraud and hacking. Not all vulnerabilities are clear yet and, as with any digital technology, there is an arms race between those that wish to defend and those that wish to attack.

In this sense, it is of major concern that necessary safety measures have been taken (automated and otherwise), that regular audits take place, and that pentests are performed so that the ledger remains secure. Other risks come out of the type of blockchain technology you are using. As there are many different kinds out there, they each have advantages and disadvantages. Sometimes transactions are irreversible, counterparties are hidden, transaction amounts can disappear, private keys can never be recovered, and so on. This means that, as always, you shouldn't look at distributed ledgers as a magical solution. Risks are inherent in any technology and you have to understand what the capabilities are to find the right use case. An example is the blockchain-based tool launched by Armanino.[12] Traditional techniques are still necessary to gain the final report, but intermediary audits can be automated.

---

[11]www2.deloitte.com/mt/en/pages/audit/articles/mt-blockchain-a-game-changer-for-audit.html
[12]www.coindesk.com/accounting-firms-blockchain-tool-claims-to-perform-a-30-second-audit

Accountancy

In line with auditing, blockchain technology could have a major impact on accountancy. As the technology itself is often described as a distributed ledger, the connection is clear. The technology finds its roots in transactions, ownership, and a ledger of financial information. Accounting platforms with an underlying blockchain-like distributed ledger technology could change the future of the industry. For this to function, there is a clear need for standards and regulations. If we could achieve this, the need for reconciliation and conflict management could be reduced to the bare minimum.[13] Blockchain would also increase the transparency of financial information and could have a major impact on the timeliness of transactions. Fraud could, in a similar sense, be reduced. "Cooking the books" is much harder when you are dealing with immutable transactions and multiple participants who need to verify and confirm these transactions. Also, classic "human error: could easily be detected and filtered out of the ledgers, as the other participants could recognize and reject it.

One organization promoting the possible opportunities in tax, accountancy, and auditing is the Accounting Blockchain Coalition. It has many partners working together to achieve this goal.[14]

Insurance

An industry that isn't famous for fast innovation in its way of working is the insurance industry.[15] However, the initial interest in blockchain technology came from the financial sector, so the insurers were naturally pushed to look into the technology and possible innovation opportunities as well. This industry has to deal with many challenges, such as the stringent and often complex compliance and legal frameworks in which they operate. There is the limited growth that is achievable in the mature markets, the interest rates as they are in many countries, fraudulent claims that need to be processed and investigated, third-party payment transactions that must be verified, data that needs to be processed, and the administrative burden resting on many of these companies. We can also add the pressure to come up with new products to deal with the challenges of the modern world, new compensation modes depending on the scheme that is being put in place, and so on. Finally, we also have to look into the security of the data being processed, as this is a concern for any major industry dealing with personal data. In a broader aspect, data is

---

[13]www.icaew.com/technical/technology/blockchain/blockchain-articles/blockchain-and-the-accounting-perspective
[14]https://accountingblockchain.net/
[15]www.idginsiderpro.com/article/3301163/how-blockchain-is-disrupting-the-insurance-industry-for-the-better.html

also necessary for the reserve calculations based on their current contracts. This is of key importance in the insurance space, when exposures must be rebalanced considering certain risks in their portfolios. When you look at all these points, you can see why the industry is facing many challenges.

Blockchain might not be a magical answer, but it could be one of the tools that brings insurance companies into the modern age. A first obvious case is that of fraud prevention.[16] This affects the business and the final consumer, simply because insurance companies need to deal with fraud and that affects the bottom line. With blockchain platforms, there could be more coordination between the insurers on the market. At this time, each insurer is performing analysis on the data they have, so they might filter out suspicious claims or activity. If insurers could work together and share data that is essential to filter out fraud cases (as insurance fraud can often be turned from company to company), the cost might be shared between all the participants while the success rate increases.

This is, of course, strongly linked to data and this is the second place where it might really help the insurance industry. It could help both with the quality of the data as with data management. Currently, a lot of insurers are struggling to deal with the vast amounts of data they have to process while they want to provide better services to their clients. Blockchain technology might also help to improve the current data management systems for the better.

Other opportunities can be found in the underlying payment systems and claims processing, as a lot can be done via automated smart contracts. This, in combination with machine learning models, could help filter out the suspicious cases, while those that are considered "normal" could be processed smoothly without any extra cost for the insurance company itself. This would lead to a better customer experience as they can immediately validate their claims. At the same it could reduce the overhead and administrative costs that insurers deal with.

In the same vein, there is a final important possibility, which focuses on product development and offerings to prospective clients.[17] Effective data management of a blockchain platform could enhance actuarial models as they are in use today, which in turn can help develop new contract terms, better suited for the client.

As you might imagine, a lot of startups have jumped at the opportunity to fill the gap when it comes to the insurance industry and blockchain technology. An interesting example is Estua-re, which is a platform launched by Legal and

---

[16]https://medium.com/datadriveninvestor/blockchain-can-revolutionise-the-insurance-industry-896555e0a7d5

[17]www.dataversity.net/blockchain-in-the-insurance-industry-what-to-expect-in-the-future/#

General Reinsurance Plc.[18] The reinsurance platform is used for pension risk transfer execution and can handle pricing, claims, financial reporting, and collateral.[19]

A second example is Everledger. Everledger offers several solutions, but one of them is focused on the insurance industry. They want to increase transparency and allow for automation, trust, and increased accuracy. The solution also helps with fraud identification.

Other startups in the insurance space include Etherisc[20], which focuses on process improvement solutions and cuts down on processing fees and claim-processing times. Guardtime[21] is a developer that goes much broader than insurance alone, but has developed a maritime insurance platform with Maersk. FidentiaX[22] a marketplace for tradable insurance policies. Of course, there are many more out there and others in development, but this gives you a good idea of how development is going and where we might see new solutions in the future. No industry remains untouched and we will see major changes in the years to come when we look at the insurance industry.

Real Estate

Real estate (and certainly commercial real estate) is another market that might change due to the influence of blockchain technology in the coming years. Many transactions that now require the interference of one or more third parties could possibly be automated by using smart contracts on top of a blockchain platform. Think of any transaction that leads to the purchase or sale of a property, leasing contracts, and financing and management transactions.[23]

Where do we commonly find the biggest issues with the existing real estate industry? First of all, it is not open to everyone.[24] It shouldn't be too hard to understand that the most important barrier are the funds necessary to acquire real estate. This has always been a very high barrier but it is not the only one. Most countries have very stringent rules when it comes to real estate and how one can acquire it: identification, credit score, financing, notary services, cash requirements, accreditation, proof of income, access to sponsors, and so on.

---

[18]www.legalandgeneralgroup.com/media-centre/press-releases/legal-general-reinsurance-launches-world-s-first-pension-risk-transfer-prt-blockchain-reinsurance-platform/
[19]www.everledger.io/
[20]https://etherisc.com/
[21]https://guardtime.com/
[22]www.fidentiax.com/
[23]www2.deloitte.com/us/en/pages/financial-services/articles/blockchain-in-commercial-real-estate.html
[24]https://blockgeeks.com/guides/blockchain-real-estate/

Even in the world of commercial real estate, there are certain requirements we need to deal with. Due diligence processes need to take place to make sure that all legal, operational, and investment implications are clear. Brokers act between investment parties to provide the right information to the right people. The number of third parties you have to rely on seems endless and often this is fixed in law, so there is no way around it. A second issue, closely tied to the first one, is the lack of transparency in the entire process. People who enter the real estate market for the first time often discover, to their dismay, how difficult it is to do everything right. And you have to consider all the middlemen you need to trust to give you the correct information.

With the use of a distributed ledger, you can improve the property search process, expedite pre-lease due diligence, ease cash flow management, and allow for easier and more transparent property title management. Information can and should be free for everyone when considering something as crucial as commercial real estate. The process shouldn't be unnecessarily difficult considering the investment many families are making when it comes to acquiring real estate. In the same vein, you should be certain that everything is in line with regulation when acquiring property. You want to know if the owner selling the property is really the owner, that the building meets current regulations, that there are no other claims on the property, and so on. This can all be determined using a blockchain-enabled platform that could open up the information to all participants. The lack of transparency also leads to many possibilities for corruption, tax evasion, money laundering, and worse. When looking into reports from Global Financial Integrity, one can see that between China and the U.S. alone, there was a flow of 1 trillion USD between 2002 and 2011 that involved New York real estate.[25] In the fight against corruption and financial crime, distributed ledger could lead to more open information sources, discouraging individuals from spending their illicit money on real estate. All of this also creates a strain on the speed of the process, which can easily take months and, in case of international real estate, years.

We mentioned before the high costs associated with acquiring real estate. There is not only the cost of real estate itself to consider, but also the other fees that are linked to acquiring property. Taxes, notary fees, processing fees, transfer fees, exchange fees, broker fees, investment costs, and so on wear down many investors entering the market. By weeding out the middlemen, these costs could also be reduced to the absolute minimum.

Of course, these ideas aren't new and are well-spread throughout the world, which has led to a number of startups using blockchain technology to change the real estate market. One of these startups is called PropertyClub[26] and it wants to increase the transparency in the real estate market and make it easier for people looking for property in NYC.

---

[25]https://gfintegrity.org/chinas-corrupt-economic-fugitives-finding-home-us/
[26]https://propertyclub.nyc/

Another is Managego, which focuses on property owners in the real estate market. It digitizes rent payments, maintenance requests, rental applications, and more.[27] Another startup that has an interesting approach to the real estate market is called Meridio.[28] It wants to make real estate more tradable by making it divisible with equity. This way, ownership of real estate can be shared by many investors and these shares can be traded on top of their platform. At the same time, this reduces transaction costs and lowers the investment minimums necessary to enter the market. Many other startups exist that have an alternative approach to the real estate market, but the key takeaway is that blockchain technology can help improve the current challenges that are faced by market's participants. Whether you believe in the technology or not, these startups are here to stay and will change the current market processes.

The Legal Industry

The legal industry is a notoriously slow one when it comes to change and innovation. A lot of their practices are almost set in stone when it comes to procedures. However, the pressure of blockchain technology is mounting and startups are trying to revolutionize the landscape so that there might be real change for all participants. Why is there always pressure when it comes to the application of new technologies in the legal sector? Because there is always the question of what the legal consequences are of applying a certain technology. This means that the very application of distributed ledgers might have an impact on the legal outcome of a process. In no other industry is there such a fundamental question when it comes to the application of new technologies. In itself, this leads to legal discussions that can seem endless. In essence, there are changes needed in the very laws themselves for many countries so that blockchain technology can actually be applied. When I say that legal changes are necessary, this means that there is a need for clear regulation, one that is not open to many interpretations. If there is an open interpretation, it should be in the sense that the application of new procedures and technologies are supported.

Another important aspect that we need to consider is the legal industry itself when you enter as an outside participant. All of us come into contact with the legal profession some time in our lives at key moments. Lawyers, notaries, legal clerks and judges, depending on the situation we are facing, help us with many processes such as marriage, divorce, buying a house, and dealing with the passing of a loved one. The procedures are often unclear to participants who aren't familiar with the legal profession, let alone understanding the stipulations of any decisions they make. On top of that, the costs of legal representation are often quite high. This leads to even more frustration and hesitation to call upon a legal professional in time of need.

---

[27]https://managego.com/
[28]www.meridio.co/

Law firms have also witnessed change over the last couple of years. Depending on the branch of law one specializes in, the "classic" family office isn't what it used to be. Major legal firms are moving in and vying for contracts with corporate clients.[29]

So where do we actually see the benefits of blockchain technology specifically in the legal world (as one could argue that any form of digitalization could have a major impact on the industry as a whole)? As always, the existence of smart contract functionalities could help to automate requests, legal contracts, and their outcomes. This could give rise to new products that can be offered at a lower cost. By adding descriptions that are clear for any outsider, a complete new market could be created.[30] Opening up the market for any person in need, with clear explanations and at a lower cost, could mean a democratization of the legal profession. Transparency would increase as well, as the outcome of legal contracts could be clearly defined in a fixed set. One would no longer be able to disagree about the existence of a contract or the possible outcomes. In this vein, blockchain platforms could help current disputes concerning intellectual property rights by clearly defining who the owner of certain IP is and how the rights can be transferred to another party. This information can be made public so that there can be no dispute and all parties can act in transparency without the need for a third party.

A final obvious point where the legal industry and the blockchain world touch on each other is the technology itself. The existence of ICOs, cryptocurrencies, and open investment mechanisms has opened up an entire new world. Although there have been a lot of new opportunities, as always, there are also people taking advantage of the situation. This has led to cases of clear theft or misinformation to investors. As there is often not yet a clear legal framework for the technology and all its possibilities, lawyers who familiarize themselves with the concept could help shape the world of tomorrow.[31] Notable examples relating to smart contracts are the states Arizona and Tennessee in the U.S. which have accepted the digital signature of smart contracts as legally binding.[32,33]

One of the startups that has jumped to this opportunity is Legal Nodes.[34] Surprisingly, it claims to be GDPR compliant, as it includes several legal, organizational, and technical measures to achieve this goal (although they don't specify what this means). Their platform can be used for legal support, M&A deals, corporate structuring, and legal assistance. Another important

---

[29]https://blogs.thomsonreuters.com/legal-uk/2019/11/15/use-of-the-cloud-is-on-the-rise-in-law-firms/
[30]https://consensys.net/enterprise-ethereum/use-cases/law/
[31]www.disruptordaily.com/blockchain-use-cases-legal/
[32]www.coindesk.com/arizona-governor-signs-blockchain-bill-law
[33]https://publications.tnsosfiles.com/acts/110/pub/pc0591.pdf
[34]https://legalnodes.org/

advocate of blockchain technology is called Empowered Law[35] and it strives for public records on blockchain platforms to make them easily accessible. Other clear opportunities lie in notary services, which are essential for almost any society to function. With the advent of new technologies the almost ancient profession could see a complete change in the way of working, user friendliness, and cost. Finally, there is also the possibility of optimizing corporate filings. An example is IBM, which has become Delaware's future blockchain provider when it comes to their new corporate filing system.[36] It could lower the cost, increase transparency, and automate processing.

Supply Chain

You might not immediately see it, but supply chain offers a clear use case for blockchain technology. It's not really a specific industry, but is a collection of people, businesses, and different industries that interact when it comes to supply chain. More often than not, it entails an entire network of suppliers, transportation companies, vendors, and customers that interact once or in a more permanent way, and this is irrespective of region. As this is a fundamental element in any industry today, there are many reasons to be critical of the existing processes and procedures. It is often an expensive process, with a lot of delays due to inefficient processes and procedures, being inflexible to change in demand, and based on the more legacy ways of working. Certainly, if we look at new techniques that are revolutionizing entire industries, we often see that these are lacking in current supply chain processes. As customers demand a better experience, more on-demand products and services, flexibility, and quick resolutions to problems, there are major changes to come.

As I have stated multiple times, the blockchain technology isn't a magical solution that simply fixes all of these problems. But it might be one of the technologies that helps push necessary changes that aren't happening today. As always a major focus may lie on the cost reduction in current supply chain processes due to inefficiencies. By eliminating third parties and directly working together, costs can be reduced by transparent sharing of information and making sure that several payments between bank accounts don't need to happen. Smart contracts might be a valuable solution, which can be triggered when a delivery has taken place. Linked to this issue is the collection and sharing of data among the parties involved in the supply chain process.[37] Data

---

[35]https://empoweredlaw.com/
[36]https://eu.delawareonline.com/story/news/2018/07/03/ state-awards-738-000-single-bid-blostate-awards-738-000-single-bid- blockchain-cckchain-contract-ibm/751001002/
[37]https://hackernoon.com/how-blockchain-is-revolutionizing- the-supply-chain-industry-ghw83v0m

cannot be shared efficiently and integrated among the different partners in a certain supply chain, leading to the loss of valuable information needed to improve the process but also to make sure that no products are lost. Continuing with this trend is the use of EDI (Electronic Data Interchange) systems, which send information in batches to other parties. This information is shared at certain intervals, which leads to issues relating to the change in pricing or when shipments go missing.

For all of these issues, the use of blockchain technology might greatly improve the current supply chain processes. One company that has understood that is Coca-Cola. In collaboration with SAP, they created a blockchain solution in the U.S. for their supply chain.[38] Coke One North America (CONA) works currently with 70 manufacturers on their blockchain solution for the 160,000 bottles that are delivered daily to shops in the U.S. By improving the process, orders can be reduced from processes that take up to months to only a couple of days. Another major company is Walmart. They have teamed up with IBM specifically for their food supply chains.[39] Currently, they track Chinese pork and Mexican mangoes, but one could easily see the potential for the future.

Several platforms have been developed to aid the supply chain industry to make sure that blockchain integration can be performed with ease. Insolar[40] offers the use of private and public blockchains. This provides the most options for possible integration, as it leaves migration to other solutions open. Other startups that focus on supply chain are Skuchain, which aims to improve the security and visibility in the global supply chain process; SyncFab, which focuses on purchase order management; Shipchain, which focuses on freight transport smart contracts; and Origintrail, which offers a data exchange protocol for interconnected supply chains.

Resources

In line with what you might expect from supply chain processes, pharmaceutical supply chains and the energy trade, there are also possibilities to optimize the mining and general industry markets. An example is BHP Billiton, which has chosen to use blockchain technology to record the movements of rock and fluid samples to better secure the data that is being generated and reported for the delivery of these minerals.[41]

---

[38]https://nieuws.btcdirect.eu/blockchain-coca-cola/
[39]https://fortune.com/2017/08/22/walmart-blockchain-ibm-food-nestle-unilever-tyson-dole/
[40]https://insolar.io/
[41]www.supplychain247.com/article/worlds_largest_mining_company_to_use_blockchain_for_supply_chain

A second example relates to the diamond market, where precious stones often tend to find origin in conflict areas. The term "blood diamond" isn't familiar to everyone, and it refers to the fact that these stones are used to fuel conflicts everywhere in the world. They promote child labor, child soldiers, and various war crimes that I am not going to discuss in detail. By using distributed ledgers, we could help verify the origin of these diamonds and precious stones, ensuring that with the purchase of these stones, we do not promote such violence against humanity. The De Beers are responsible for about 30% of the mines, trades, and markets of diamonds, and they have chosen to implement a blockchain solution to help trace stones from their very origins to the customers who buy them.[42] By doing this, the platform can become another measure in the fight against these crimes.

One final example in this context is the startup Everledger.[43] Everledger has developed several industry applications that focus on diamonds, gemstones, minerals, wines, luxury products, and art. They wish to improve the transparency in these markets, to allow for clear compliance processes and trust between all parties. By creating unique identities, one can no longer doubt where these resources come from.

Risk Management and Cybersecurity

It is certainly worth asking how the risk management and cybersecurity sector could be influenced by the introduction of the blockchain technology. Whether or not you believe in the technology and the possible applications, the fact is that companies are trying new ways of working with distributed ledgers, applications, and platforms. This already means that there will be an impact on risk and security. With the advent of new technologies, new vulnerabilities are introduced and they need to be examined and tested. This calls upon professionals who not only understand the technology and its applications, but also can edit the code to discover how it might be used with malicious intent. Depending on the application, these risks can be linked to operational, credit, or liquidity risk (and in some cases even market risk). Again, understanding the application and the possible risks is critical.

However, there are possible advantages to the technology as well. When we look at data, some of the key characteristics in a compliance/security setting is the availability, confidentiality, and integrity of the data. Distributed ledgers could meet help all three of these requirements, as the integrity can be easily verified by storing hashes. A simple change will lead to a completely different hash so that everyone knows that the integrity of the data has been

---

[42]www.forbes.com/sites/bernardmarr/2018/03/14/how-blockchain-could-end-the-trade-in-blood-diamonds-an-incredible-use-case-everyone-should-read/#35b64c23387d
[43]www.everledger.io/industry-applications

compromised. When applied correctly, blockchain platforms could also improve data security and assure that only those participants with the necessary rights can access the data. Finally, availability can be improved, as there will no longer be a single point of failure. Each node has a copy of the data, so that when a node goes down, participants can contact the other available nodes to access the data.

In the field of data compliance, regulations often stipulate that one has to be able to prove that data hasn't been altered or changed. With immutable records stored on a distributed ledger, this can easily be achieved.[44] Tampering with data can be prevented and even in cases when data changes are possible, immutable logs show who the culprits are.

With an increase in data control and transparency, one could say that client's oversights could be improved as well. An example is the financial services industry, where the KYC (Know Your Customer) program is a well-known process in which the client needs to be identified. This identification has to pass through several steps. The cost of the entire process is high, and such is the burden on both the financial institutions and the customer. Digitalization could help because smart contracts can automate the steps of the information gathering process, and when there is a conflict, it can automatically alert internal departments or the customer that extra data validation is needed. While the process is still a necessary pain (to protect both the financial services industry and the customers), it could be improved in terms of data integrity, case handling, and testing. Anti-money laundering processes are another viable candidate for optimization via the use of blockchain technology. There are already several startups in the field looking at these processes, such as KYC Chain[45] and Tradle.[46] Customer data could be made available to regulators, including updates on any information in real-time. These processes are of course only part of the broader client onboarding program that is of major importance, which again could become a lot friendlier for future customers.

Another possible candidate is the "proof of process," where the numbers are checked to see if they really are what they appear to be. By providing step-by-step information and verification of the data, fraud can be prevented in an effective way, thus protecting customers and investors from schemes. Several startups are working on applications, such as Coinfirm[47] and QRC Group.[48]

A third example is the proof of ownership and the chain of custody, which is very important in many industries and processes. By providing immutable records in a transparent way, this information could be used to facilitate many

---

[44]www.disruptordaily.com/blockchain-use-cases-compliance/
[45]https://kyc-chain.com/
[46]https://tradle.io/
[47]www.coinfirm.com/
[48]www.qrc.group/

processes that currently are prone to fraud or at least are opaque for any outsider looking in. A company that is looking into this topic is called HyperProof.[49]

Of course, most of these initiatives look at the qualitative aspect of risk/compliance management, but it shouldn't be too difficult to understand that quantitative professionals will also feel the influence of the blockchain technology. With better data, better models can be created that reflect the reality in a much more significant way. Include the fact that you can actually link data to automated processing via smart contracts and in some cases even to entire mathematical models, you can see that the process can be optimized and become less prone to human errors.

When we consider the advantages of the blockchain technology to cybersecurity, we can also consider several points. One is the possibility to prevent access fraud by creating identities on a distributed ledger platform. Currently, the Central Authorities (CAs) in the Public Key Infrastructure (PKI) model can do this.[50] People tend to use passwords, which are generally easy to guess or hack. This leads to persistent security issues for many companies. In a sense, using a centralized database, this creates a target for hackers if they wish to steal information. One could argue that a decentralized PKI is more secure when it comes to storing such information. Another possibility in the field of cybersecurity is the use of blockchain platforms for DNS servers, thereby making the network more resilient against DDoS attacks, which are aimed at bringing down the centralized part of a DNS service. Take away this centralized part, and you can hope to take away the power of the attacker.

Energy Markets

Without a doubt, a very interesting use case for the blockchain technology are the energy markets. By using these new techniques, one can obtain a more sustainable market that more efficiently uses resources and ensures that everyone has access to this market. High costs for what is seen as a basic utility is still an issue today and a distributed ledger platform could lower costs and be beneficial for the producers, distributers, and customers.[51] According to some reports, the blockchain in energy markets could grow to 3 billion USD by 2025.[52]

---

[49]https://hyperproof.io/

[50]https://blog.capterra.com/benefits-of-blockchain-cybersecurity/

[51]https://consensys.net/enterprise-ethereum/use-cases/energy-and-sustainability/

[52]www.smart-energy.com/industry-sectors/energy-grid-management/blockchain-in-energy-market-to-reach-3-billion-by-2025/

We could see the use of distributed ledger platforms popping up for P2P energy trading and decentralized marketplaces, which make sure that energy as a scarce resource is used most efficiently in a price-effective way. As the sector is already accustomed to innovation, with solar energy, electric vehicles, smart meters, and more coming in the future, the blockchain technology could become an integral part of this change. In the sense of sustainability and resources coming from acceptable sources, tracking these sources could help adapt the market as it exists today.

However, "classic" energy sectors stand to gain as well. The petroleum and gas trades have many actors, and as with any supply chain, cost reduction, trade optimization, and transparency can be achieved via blockchain platforms. It is also a heavily regulated market with sanctions on several countries that produce these products. To ensure that petroleum or gas is not coming from a sanctioned area, distributed ledger technology could provide immutable proof of where the resources came from. Reporting about energy data and how it's being used could also be improved. An example is the Chilean government, which is using a blockchain technology to store and report energy data.

With the energy market being a global market, cross-border engagement could be improved in regions such as the EU. It could help to share information across state borders, allow for commodity trading in a cost-effective way, creating real-time data repositories and more. By moving renewable energy to the global market, such as the classic energy resources, it could help change the world as a whole for the better.

The Banking Industry

We have already stated it several times—the birth of blockchain technology took place at the time of the banking crisis in 2008. It was meant as a protest and as a possible solution to work completely around the financial industry as a whole. It is only natural that those same banks have shown a very deep interest in the technology and its possible applications. This also means that this industry has seen the most use cases so far and as such can share the most experience in both success and failure.

There is still a lot of enthusiasm in the industry for new and future applications, but they have learned from their past mistakes and will not simply jump to any new ventures without considering the possible risks or other implementations. Key issues that troubled banks in the past have been the difficulty of scaling solutions for larger commercial adoption without clogging up the entire network, which would lead to customer frustration and eventually customers fleeing the platform. There have also been issues with the ongoing regulatory uncertainty that surrounds the blockchain technology, which makes further investments in related projects risky.

The most difficult aspect, as always, has been to bring several parties together to work on a platform. For competitors to work together, a very good understanding of the reasons why this could be beneficial for all is important. This is not always easy. If we take as an example the banking industry in Belgium and the open banking regulation, the smaller competitors worked together to deliver a compliant and similar open API platform, which makes it easier for third parties to work together. The bigger players, on the other hand, each chose their own path, which eventually made it more expensive for third parties to integrate with all of them. This was in sharp contrast to the Scandinavian region, where, even across borders, the majority of the banking scene was able to implement a similar platform. These lessons of the past teach us that it is easier to work with the smaller players (perhaps they have more to win from enhanced customer services and reduced costs) as well as a cultural aspect where certain countries have banks that work together with one another more readily for the benefit of all.

Leading banks all over the world have been working together to figure out how this technology could optimize their current way of working. One exciting field is money transfers for remittances. Sending money abroad has always been a pain. They are not only expensive but often prove to be cumbersome. Blockchain technology could ease this cost.

Other processes that might be improved by using blockchain technology is that of anti-money laundering and the "know your customer" processes, where fraud can be reduced. Identity can be verified, the process can easily be audited, and the validity of documents can be ensured via distributed ledgers. These processes are often a pain for customers, but when a shared platform could be created, the customer could decide which financial institutions get access to the information. This would mean that the customer would have to go through the entire process only once, after which all his financial institutions would have access to the same info. Updating the information could require the same streamlined process, reducing the impact on the customer.

Financial inclusion has also been an important argument for the creation of financial services over blockchain platforms. Low prices because of automation on top of the platform allow for a broader client base. At the same time, everything necessary for the client can easily be performed via a smartphone. This might still prove to be a barrier, but it is a less harsh one than a personal computer. Digital IDs linked to your smartphone can be used, where otherwise identifying a customer might prove to be next to impossible.

All over the world, new projects are being launched and tested to improve the money and credit markets. The promise that blockchain made the financial industry over night has proven to be a lie. Still, there is a lot of potential that remains untapped and that can be used to revolutionize the industry as a whole. While we might have landed at a moment of "blockchain fatigue" in the financial industry, similar to the AI winters of the past where AI was no longer popular, I remain confident that this technology will come back and further improve the banking industry.

Financial Instruments

We mentioned a bit earlier that the blockchain world has also seen a rise in new financial products. We do need to state immediately that the local financial authority has the power to determine what a legal financial instrument is in a certain country. For some countries, these definitions are quite broad, while others have tried to keep cryptospace as far as possible from customers to protect them from possible losses.

In Germany, for example, the legal definition has been adopted as follows since March 2, 2020: "Digital representation of a value that has not been issued or guaranteed by any central bank or public body and is not necessarily linked to a currency specified by law and that does not have the legal status of a currency or money, but is accepted as a medium of exchange by natural or legal persons and can be transmitted, stored, and traded electronically."[53] This provides a very broad base to possible instruments but also imposes stark requirements when considering the supervisory programs and compliance needed to ensure that the right investments are recommended for the right customer, so that risk-averse customers don't end up with risky investments.

It is this same, often uncertain, regulatory environment that has proven to be a barrier for further innovation. This is a double-edged sword, as new instruments could help those without access to regular financial services to finance their lives and increase profits. On the other hand, widening the door to instruments that are often not well understood can lead to higher risks (as both the banking crisis of 2008 and the cryptocrash of 2018 have shown us).

When working together, regulatory instances from all over the world could come to similar terms, thereby reducing the regulatory uncertainty and creating a stable ground for new financial instruments. Later in this book you will read an entire section on cryptocurrency regulation, which really shows the difference in interpretation when it comes to cryptocurrencies.

It's interesting to know that there are now also investment funds focusing on cryptocurrencies. Lending instruments, put and call options, and automated contracts have all been introduced.

---

[53]https://bitcoinist.com/crypto-now-officially-seen-as-financial-instruments-in-germany/

Outside of the Finance World

Even though the blockchain technology will be forever linked to finance and the financial industry for many people, this doesn't mean that there aren't opportunities or possibilities outside of the blockchain technology. One could take a look at many different industries or departments, but the following sections list just a few so that you have an idea of how people are using distributed ledgers in new and innovative ways.

The Media

An important sector in which the blockchain technology might prove its worth is the world of media and news.[54] We have seen several examples in the last couple of years where fake news affected the behavior of people in harmful ways. These are often directed attempts to discredit certain political parties or individuals. They have also been used to direct political decisions and attack the reputation of major companies. A more recent example of fake news and its negative influence on the world is that of the Coronavirus. Online, several conspiracy theories spread. One stated that the government was responsible for the spread of the Coronavirus, so that tags could be vaccinated into people and tracked via 5G. Another stated that 5G suppresses the immune system and yet another stated that the Coronavirus spread certain radio waves themselves, which it uses to communicate to one another. This led to people in the UK, the Netherlands, and other countries to set fire to the 5G masts. This example shows how dangerous fake news can be and that combating these techniques should be a priority of everyone.

Blockchain platforms can offer traceability, transparency, and security when it comes to news articles. It could not only help to verify the source of certain articles, but also allow participants to flag articles as fake news, hence forcing out those that would abuse the (decentralized) network and prove the value of the information that is being spread. *The New York Times* Company is testing the blockchain technology to combat fake news and misinformation.[55] The proof of concept they currently have stores metadata of photos and videos such as data, place of the image, person who took the shot, how it was edited, and how it was eventually published. Another company using distributed ledgers to fight fake news is Orange. You might not immediately imagine a telecoms operator focusing on fake news, but as a major operator in the communication process, they have seen and understood that they play a

---

[54]www.leewayhertz.com/blockchain-fake-news/
[55]www.coindesk.com/new-york-times-confirms-its-using-blockchain-to-combat-fake-news

major role in spreading fake news.[56] Orange worked together with the startup called Block Expert to create the application called safe.press.[57]

The safe.press application allows you to check the source of an article, so that you can verify if the article you are reading is reliable. One could still try to defraud the source, but this is very interesting step in the move to secure information. It is not the only one of its kind, so it will be interesting to see how these applications evolve over time. Again, you shouldn't be blind to the possible downsides of this technology. If a country controls the Internet use of its citizens and controls all the sources of news, it would in fact control all information its citizens are receiving through the majority of its sources.

The possibilities of the blockchain technology within media are of course broader.[58] We are currently experiencing the rise (and fall) of multiple platforms that allow anyone with a computer and an Internet connection to participate in the media sector. This doesn't take away that there are still major players that actually control the market. This leads to uneven compensation for the actual creators of content. With blockchain-based platforms, all creators can receive direct compensation for the use of their content and property. This can also be used to track the authorized viewers, usage of content, transfer of ownership, and smart contracts that can manage the entire process, end to end. This effectively eliminates the need to work with third parties that are often not compensating the creators as they should be.

There are many startups that have seen these opportunities and entered the media industry with specific solutions. We mentioned earlier in this books startups such as Ujo Team, Opus Foundation, and Stem, which focus on the streaming industry in particular. They offer channels for independent music distribution, freedom for the artists when it comes to compensation, automating royalty payments in general, and allowing for the contact with their fans in open and distributed ways so that none of them can be blocked from content.

Another important topic in the media industry is that of intellectual property rights and certainly how these can be protected in the modern age. Piracy is nothing new and most people are aware of how they can get a free copy of almost anything. The blockchain technology could not only help manage the authorized users who have access to certain content, but could also help manage and timestamp everything. This would effectively prevent any attempts of tampering during any step of the process. Startups such as Mediachain and Monegraph focus on the subject and want to empower the creators.

---

[56]www.ledgerinsights.com/orange-blockchain-fake-news/
[57]https://safe.press/
[58]https://hackernoon.com/blockchain-a-new-solution-for-the-media-and-entertainment-industry-f8c83ad3dc07

We should also consider public events that require the purchase of a ticket. Each year there are many attempts to commit fraud in this regard. In this vein, there are also a great many attempts in the sale of pirated merchandising. As we previously mentioned, the blockchain technology can provide an extra layer of authenticity.[59]

The Health Sector

The health sector might not be the first sector you think of when considering implementations using the blockchain technology.[60] The idea of sensitive personal data locked away in some database, which can be accessed by anyone, should make you think. Still, the blockchain technology could have a major impact on how the healthcare industry is functioning today. The industry is not known for fast innovation when it comes to the general functioning of hospitals and the administrative burden that is often part of the patient relationship.[61] To this day, it still happens that patients register at different hospitals when they aren't happy with the diagnosis they receive. The studies are repeated at multiple hospitals but these are often unaware of some research that has happened at other institutions. There are efforts in place to remove these barriers, but it still remains an issue. The major risk here is the patient's well-being.

So where do we find two major areas of concern? The identification of patients and the blocking of information. There is no universal patient identifier to this day, so that mistaken identity can still happen. Linked to this is the blocking of information, as it can lead to problems in the care for the patient. Information is often not shared between institutions, there are difficulties when data is requested, a long procedures, long waiting times, and so on. Sometimes the patients themselves try to hide information, leading to their own harm. Even though this information should be available to medical professionals and certainly should be shared upon request of the patient, this is often not the case. Another linked issue is that hospitals and other institutions often have limited funds and data security isn't a priority. This leaves very sensitive data open for possible breaches, where in turn people could become victim of this shared information. A private distributed ledger solution might be the solution to these now common problems.[62]

When we use such a platform, we can create unique identities so that there can no longer be a case of mistaken identity or mismatched patient data. We could actually reduce the number of medical mistakes. In the same vein, medical fraud and abuse could be halted as everything is recorded in a

[59]www.entrepreneur.com/article/333856
[60]https://blockgeeks.com/guides/blockchain-in-healthcare/
[61]www.healtheuropa.eu/blockchain-the-trust-solution-for-healthcare/96840/
[62]https://blockgeeks.com/guides/blockchain-in-healthcare/

tamper-free database, making sure that each action taken is there for everyone to see. You could give patients complete control over their data to share with those people and institutions they wish. On the other hand, if a medical practitioner wants to verify that other data exists on the patient, they can do so. Will they immediately get access to the data? Depending on the setup, no. But if they ask the patient for that information and the patient refuses to share the information, the medical practitioner has to take the proper precautions for the sake of the patient. An example is the Opioid epidemic, where patients fake injury, injure themselves, or try to collect drugs at several institutions for the same injury.[63] Only with proper information sharing can patients be protected and can abuse be halted. Patients could also receive rewards via a reward mechanism linked to the blockchain platform, incentivizing them to follow a healthy lifestyle, follow a care plan, or take action to remain healthy.

Another major aspect of the health sector is the pharma industry, which is a major industry. A lot of medicine is sold each day and some of this supply ends up in the wrong hands. There is also the fabrication of other products that aren't really from the supplier but end up somewhere in the middle of the sales process and put patients in harm's way. Counterfeit drugs alone cost the pharma industry $200 billion, so you can understand that this is a major issue. The goal is to reduce the impact of these counterfeit drugs in terms of cost and also reduce the major risks many people are subject to because of these drugs.

A blockchain platform could validate the existence of certain drugs when they are being transported. In the same sense a lot of pharmaceuticals are returned by wholesalers for a variety of reasons.[64] Often these drugs aren't destroyed but instead are resold. Before this second sale can happen, the authenticity of the pharmaceuticals needs to be verified to make sure that they are the the same drugs. The EU has the Falsified Medicine Directive, which requires drugs to be serialized/barcoded and uploaded in a centralized database. In the U.S. and other countries, this isn't the case, so again a blockchain application might have a positive impact on the market. In the same way, one could prevent counterfeit drugs being sold, as these would not verified in the system.

Blockchain could also be used to verify the consent that a patient gives for clinical trials data, as well as the validity of the test outcomes. This not only to verify the outcome of the study but also to make sure that the well-being of the test subject is respected at all times. A startup that focuses on this very topic is called Clinico.[65]

---

[63]www.hhs.gov/opioids/about-the-epidemic/index.html
[64]https://medium.com/blockchainbistro/top-5-use-cases-of-blockchain-in-pharma-and-healthcare-that-you-should-know-about-77ccdd76369b
[65]www.cliniko.com/

In line with the use case presented before, a distributed ledger platform could help create a universal database, which could give us a clear database with clinical trials on new drugs and medications, follow the production of drugs and medicine, and their distribution all over the world. This means that if all suppliers and vendors could be persuaded to work together in one major system, we would be able to phase out a lot of counterfeit drugs due to the simple fact that the data in the blockchain is tamper free, and processors in the middle cannot simply adapt the data to their liking. With every action being clearly logged, no person could deny involvement in fraud or the production of counterfeit products.

Insurance fraud specifically in the healthcare sector is another concern. An interesting startup that takes a look into this is called ALLIVE.[66] Here data can be shared with insurers based on the requests made by the client and this can be linked to a validation by a medical professional. This way, the fraudulent participant must have at least a few accomplices to succeed, and their cooperation is logged away in the blockchain for eternity.[67]

Other possible advantages include cost reduction due to the administrative burden of many hospitals. Blockchain could also enhance security and controls over healthcare transactions (one would be amazed how confidential data is sometimes processed, but this not only in the healthcare sector), improve general doctor-patient interactions, track medical transactions, and so on.

Again, we should always keep in mind what we are doing with sensitive personal data and not just blindly jump over to new solutions. These considerations determine the future of many patients and, with data protection in mind, we should move forward with a clear vision.

The Public Sector

Within the public sector, several possibilities for the implementation of blockchain and distributed ledger technology have been identified and already been used. A first aspect of the public sector that I want to highlight has to do with pensions.

Pensions are one of the major topics when elections are at the door in Europe, but also elsewhere across the globe. One of the reasons is that pensions make up a significant part of the costs that governments are dealing with. That is why we have in Belgium, but also in many other countries, the so-called *pillars*. The first pillar is what the government provides for you when you retire, the second pillar is what can be saved from your employer, and the third pillar is what you yourself voluntarily set aside.

---

[66]https://allive.io/index_en.html
[67]www.ibm.com/blogs/blockchain/2018/06/first-mover-advantage-innovation-through-blockchain/

The major problem that most countries have with their current pension schemes is that the current working population needs to pay for the retired population. This wasn't a problem in times with increasing population numbers, but with falling birth rates, this system is facing some tough challenges.

Blockchain to the rescue! If things were only that easy. But some solutions have been put forward to help at least in part with the challenges that we are currently facing. We are going to mention a couple of those solutions here.

What are people currently looking for in a pension scheme? An easy-to-comprehend system that allows participants to understand how they can secure their financial future and invest in a safe way. If possible, it should be easy, low-cost, fraud-free, and easy to understand.

Several players have entered the market just for this purpose: to help people invest in their future in a way they can trust and understand. This, of course, offers in no way a solution for the first two pillars of the system I described, but at least it allows people to have some assurance of what they can set aside for themselves.

A beautiful example is NestEgg[68], which is a blockchain-based solution in the Netherlands that allows participants to crowd-fund certain sustainable infrastructure. If the crowdfunding is successful, the infrastructure is built and you are a partial owner of said infrastructure. Each product has its own investment policy (NestEgg is linked to AGP, the largest pension fund in the Netherlands), where you can choose to reduce your energy bill or receive the return on your bank account. This way, you can slowly (you can already invest starting from 25 Euro) grow your personal savings and maintain your cost of living. At the same time, you are helping fund the infrastructure of the future.

A second project I want to highlight here is Akropolis. It also focuses on the third pillar and is directed at participants interested in creating their own, personal investment funds. In a decentralized way each participant can choose in which pension products they would like to invest. All transactions are transparent, together with the eventual fund performance. An audit of the fund can happen hassle-free.

Of course, there are many more areas in which we could consider blockchain applications when we look at the public sector. One of those areas is the concept of partnering. Whether you are in the EU or anywhere else in the world, partnerships with the private sector or between other public entities are commonplace. With the use of blockchain platforms you can create more transparency in these initiatives, which can open up opportunities and participation. It can also provide insight into how government funds are spent, how decisions are made, and what the output is of these collaborations.

---

[68]https://hackernoon.com/attempting-to-reform-the-global-pension-system-with-blockchain-21e0ab9b51d9

Where these platforms and intergovernmental partnerships now are often opaque to anyone trying to look in from the outside (and often even for the people directly involved), with distributed ledgers, these governance systems can become more transparent. It could also democratize the process when people subject to the partnerships decisions can participate and vote on the projects they want to implement, directly giving power to the citizens who are subject to the decisions being made.[69]

These platforms could also be used to reduce fraud in the sector and help manage the funds in a clear, transparent, and secure manner. By linking the funds to the blockchain technology, you can also increase compliance by implementing smart contracts that are automatically triggered if the request is compliant and sets in motion regulatory action if it isn't.[70] Other possibilities include the secure storage of government and citizen data, trusted governments, and civil online systems. These applications could reduce the costs of many of the current applications. As it is for any person whop has to deal with administrations these days, it is likely to be a hassle. Why? Most of the time, you interact with the government only when you have an issue, so that any process already seems slow and painful to start with. If you consider that a lot of these processes are indeed outdated, you start to understand the frustration that a lot of people feel, even when they only think about having to interact with the government. As the frustration is likely to stay, these applications could reduce these feelings to the bare minimum.

Identity and Voting Applications

When discussing the blockchain technology, identity is quite an important part of it. Traceability and transparency are only effective if identity within the platform can be ensured. Luckily, this can easily be done with distributed ledger applications. As with many things, voting is an integral part of life if you are living in a democracy. There are several risks linked to the voting process, as any person can understand. Fraud and deception are two of those risks. But something more general and what a lot of people might also understand is the simple frustrations that go into the process itself. Getting up early in the morning, or racing from your job to simply stand in line to wait, so that you can cast your vote. You can end up standing in line for hours due to technical difficulties, or all other citizens have the same idea as you and showing up at the last moment.[71] Of course there are also other cases where people are prevented from voting by "unknown" agents, places where votes disappear, or

---

[69]www2.deloitte.com/us/en/insights/industry/public-sector/blockchain-public-sector-applications.html
[70]https://consensys.net/enterprise-ethereum/use-cases/government-and-the-public-sector/
[71]www.thebalance.com/how-the-blockchain-will-change-how-we-vote-4012008

places where votes seem to change over time. On top of that, it has become clear that the percentage of citizens who still vote is falling (sometimes dramatically) over time.

As early as in 2012, there has been research into the possibility of using the blockchain technology for the voting process, so that it could be both more secure and more reliable for citizens.[72] If you understand the fundamentals of the blockchain technology, it shouldn't be too hard to see how the technology could improve the entire process. It could lock in votes, prove that every citizen casted their vote only once, and allow voting from people's homes. The results of the voting process could be processed much quicker than today. This would also mean that public consultations could become a process of daily life, as it could be much easier to get a vote through digital means.

Several startups have jumped at the opportunity to optimize this process and are now offering solutions (or developing solutions) that might one day replace the processes we are so familiar with today. One of these startups is called FollowMyVote.[73] The company believes in using digital and technological solutions (of which the blockchain technology is a major part) to change government elections. It's used for political party voting, collegiate voting, HOA voting, and proxy voting. It uses the BitShares platform and believes that this is the best way forward to provide reliable applications that have a predictable way of working.

A second startup with a focus on the subject is called BitCongress.[74] They released a whitepaper as early as 2016 in which they proposed their solution.[75] It uses a token-based system where participants can vote based on the number of VOTE tokens they have.

Not everyone is happy with the current progress and the use of the blockchain technology in a voting landscape. There have been several warnings that turning to digital solutions might introduce extra risks in the voting process and possibly even pose a threat to democracy.[76] So far the studies that have been reported weren't positive about Internet-based voting.[77] There are currently online votes being cast in several processes. One of these examples is the general election process in the U.S., where in 2016 there were already

[72]www.newscientist.com/article/mg21328476.500-bitcoin-online-currency-gets-new-job-in-web-security/

[73]https://followmyvote.com/

[74]www.bitcongress.org/

[75]https://themerkle.com/tamper-proof-decentralized-blockchain-voting-with-bitcongress/

[76]www.computerworld.com/article/3430697/why-blockchain-could-be-a-threat-to-democracy.html

[77]www.commoncause.org/page/email-and-internet-voting-the-overlooked-threat-to-election-security/

over 100,000 ballots being cast online. Why then is the outcome of the studies currently negative? Is this linked specifically to blockchain? Of course not. Anyone that follows the news in recent years knows and should understand the risk of data and Internet-based applications. Influencing possible voters is one thing, bombarding citizens with fake news is another, but the actual election process? With the results we have seen so far, imagine what would happen if attackers were actually able to get in there. The potential of malware and cybersecurity risks is manifold.

The blockchain technology cannot simply eliminate these risks. So rather than simply saying that we should use distributed ledgers as a base for a new and digital way of voting, distributed ledgers should be only one of several pillars that help us develop an easier and more accurate voting system. General security of the applications, privacy and integrity of the data, and reliable information for the voters are all crucial issues. We shouldn't lose sight of these key considerations before moving forward, because the possible risks if we fail to provide these might be more devastating than in any other area.

The Game Industry

In 2018 about 138 billion USD was spent on video games, making the games industry one that you should certainly not ignore.[78] Even more important is that it is an industry more than willing to dive into innovation and new technologies. Virtual reality, artificial intelligence, and the newest standards in experiencing gaming mean that blockchain can play a role in the story.

Many possibilities can be discovered when one considers this industry. Many games offer in-game purchases, to the frustration of some. Distributed ledgers could offer decentralized exchanges. If you are not familiar with gaming, it might be difficult to understand, but hacking, fraud ,and theft are real problems in this virtual world. Considering the amount of money, time, and effort that is spent to gain these assets, they are often seen as valuable as any other tangible asset. The blockchain technology could also offer a proof of ownership, protecting gamers from fraudulent participants. With a distributed ledger, hackers will no longer be able to steal property. Also the progress made by players and conversations can be stored. When certain events take place, there is proof of what happened between the participants, which means admins can provide clear resolutions. This is only a conservative view on how the blockchain technology is affecting the gaming industry.[79]

---

[78]www.cnbc.com/2018/07/18/video-game-industry-is-booming-with-continued-revenue.html

[79]www.forbes.com/sites/darrynpollock/2019/05/06/blockchain-technology-can-give-billion-dollar-gaming-industry-a-decentralized-leg-up/#4d4406866094

With the tendency to create more and more open worlds, massive multiplayer experiences, and unbound rules, the classic setup cannot fully grasp these types of games any longer. Why? Participants come from all over the world to work toward a specific goal and purpose. Centralized control is therefore no longer a positive thing. One wouldn't want to see discrimination toward any of the players. Striving toward fairness, openness, and inclusivity, distributed ledgers could offer these controls. Several experiments have been performed to see how we could evolve from centralized solutions to decentralized setups, where the players gain more control over the environment they are interacting with.

A notable example is Taurion, which is a sophisticated game of the modern age.[80] The players are in full control of the world around them. At the same time there is a specific mining system in place; experience can be gained, people can trade, fight, and so on. It is a notable example of how gaming experiences can evolve, where players gain more and more control instead of being bound to the rules of the game environment. This could make the experience even more lifelike and engaging.

Education

The sector has an important set of challenges such as the openness of the sector. It is a sound principle that everyone should have access to education. The reality is completely different. Sadly, a lot of people to this day do not have equal opportunities and cannot partake in the education system as they should. On top of that, the cost of proper education has been increasing over the years, leading to massive amounts of debt and people not being able to even start the educational track they would like to. Teachers will also tell you that there is a decline in people that are willing to positively participate in classes and in many countries there is simply a shortage of educational professionals.

However, the future isn't all bleak. There has been an interesting rise in education technology. New technologies, such as virtual reality and artificial intelligence, are easily integrated in the classroom, and there is also a place for the blockchain technology. These solutions aren't going to solve all the issues that are plaguing the educational industry, but they are changing the way knowledge is shared and might actually bring hope to a currently hard situation. The "edtech" industry[81] will reach about 94 billion USD in 2020, which shows that we should take this industry seriously.

A first way that the blockchain technology plays a major role is by issuing diplomas or certifications. More and more digital courses have become available and (often) at low or reasonable prices. The actual diplomas

---

[80]https://egamers.io/meet-taurion-the-new-crypto-mmo-game-by-xaya/
[81]https://soeonline.american.edu/blog/the-future-of-education-technology

themselves could be issued and linked to a blockchain platform. This could have several benefits. First of all, one could never argue that a student didn't achieve his diploma. Next, the student could easily share his proof with possible employers and would retain full control over his personal data. One would not be able to falsify or lie about a diploma.[82] Sharing information between educational institutions and/or the government would become a lot easier and credits, sponsorships, and results could easily be verified. At the same time, it would offer a safer way of storing this information than is currently available to many universities or schools. Many other industries are plagued by the fact that they have limited resources and cannot afford to spend a lot on cybersecurity or on storing credentials. By using distributed ledgers, they can secure this information much better.

We already touched on the subject several times, but the cost of education is high and seems to be ever increasing. Several initiatives have been created to improve the road toward a valuable degree. One is the development of the MOOC (Massive Open Online Course). There were over 101 million registered users of MOOCs in 2018, which shows that more and more people are turning in this direction for further education.[83] Here, blockchain could not only help store credentials but could use micropayments, smart contracts automating exams, tests, and course delivery, and so on. Potential lies in the way information is shared with students and library services as well. The blockchain technology could help distribute information in a more affordable and socially acceptable manner.[84]

One startup looking into education and distributed ledger technology is Disciplina.[85] It focuses on test preparation and learning.

Human Resources

The human resources or HR function has a broad and important job in any company. Communication between businesses, vendors, people, activities, and processes are all aligned by this department. Currently the newspapers are talking about the "war for talent" in many different sectors being fought by HR and recruitment professionals. One shouldn't underestimate the pressure a lot of people in the industry are feeling and, as always, we can assume that the blockchain technology could in some part ease the pain.[86]

---

[82]https://hackernoon.com/blockchain-poised-to-disrupt-education-industry-f41d6f415a3f

[83]www.classcentral.com/report/mooc-stats-2018/

[84]https://dataconomy.com/2019/01/how-will-blockchain-transform-the-education-system/

[85]https://disciplina.io/en/

[86]www.gartner.com/smarterwithgartner/5-ways-blockchain-will-affect-hr/

With the use of smart contracts, imagine that the management of in-house talent and external sourcing could be in part automated. Budget approvals could be linked to strict rules, just as authorizations and reviews are. New hires could be subject to automated testing and training. Corporate policies could be easily shared and digital signing can be verified on a blockchain platform. Background and employment checks could be verified by a simple click.

Employment contracts could in the same way be managed, stored, and shared with employees. Future changes could be managed and tracked over time. Payments and benefits could be fully automated over a blockchain platform without any human intervention, easing the payment process, proving verifiable payments, and leaving a perfect audit trail.

External talent could be contacted, signed, and paid over the same platform. In a world where working at home and teleworking have more and more become the norm in our society, they could more easily be managed. As with many other examples, blockchain could help with fraud prevention, improve the security of personal data, and give proof of existence through verification by the network's nodes.[87]

Automotive Industry

The automotive industry has an increased need for connectivity with the rise of connected vehicles, fleets, and autonomous vehicles. With these connected vehicles is the need for an infrastructure that can pick up these signals. The industry is currently researching whether the blockchain technology could serve as a clear infrastructure layer. The current problems lie in the fact that each manufacturer is creating its own competing technologies without a real standard, so these implementations are uncoordinated, incompatible, and wasteful.[88] With the implementation of more and more IoT solutions in these cars and trucks, great optimizations can be achieved when we look at fleet management, payment services, infotainment, and other services.

Blockchain could help with the management of vehicles for large enterprises. Again, transparency could be gained and the entire process of managing vehicles and verifying the origin would be simplified in this manner. You could also think about insurance and payment processes, verification of the origin of vehicles, and even KYS (know your supplier) processes, which are necessary to prove that vehicles aren't stolen and are the responsibility of the seller. In the same vein, we have to be able to verify the repairs that have happened to

---

[87]https://medium.com/swlh/hr-digital-transformation-powered-by-blockchain-27d0a5794761
[88]*MetaAnalysis of Methods for Scaling Blockchain Technology for Automotive Uses.*, Sid Masih.

a vehicle. Can we trust anyone performing these repairs? In what state was the car before these repairs? Is the correct mileage reported or not?[89] All of these questions could be answered by using distributed ledgers.

The Smartphone Industry

You might not immediately think about it, but mobile phones can be changed by using the blockchain technology. Smartphone producers from all over the world have heard the calling of the decentralized web, with one of the biggest players being Samsung.[90] The Galaxy S10 is one example that includes a secure storage system for cryptocurrency private keys. Other players are HTC with the Exodus 1, Sirin labs with Finney, and Electroneum.

As we discussed earlier when we were talking about the technological aspects of the blockchain technology, these platforms allow for decentralized applications. These applications form the basis of web 3.0. The idea is that we once again move away from centralized servers from large corporations and allow peer-to-peer technologies between the smartphones themselves. So what has stopped these applications from becoming mainstream?

Several issues, come to mind, such as scalability and regulatory uncertainty. Another issue is that, to use decentralized applications, you need to be tech savvy. If a company could get around these technical impediments, they could not only allow decentralized applications to become mainstream, but also open up a new world to customers all over the world.

---

[89]www2.deloitte.com/cn/en/pages/consumer-business/articles/blockchain-in-the-automotive-industry.html
[90]www.technologyreview.com/s/613051/what-the-hell-is-a-blockchain-phoneand-do-i-need-one/

Blockchain and Regulation: The Legal World

As blockchain entered the world with new possibilities concerning data and financial instruments, it has taken decision makers a lot of time to consider the technology and introduce regulation that is both relevant and necessary to protect people from this technology. This chapter includes a short introduction to the major concepts that are currently being debated when it comes to the distributed ledger technology.

When we look at the blockchain technology and regulation, we find ourselves in murky water. Regulation on the subject often changes all over the world. Depending on the aspect of the technology (ICOs, cryptocurrencies, distributed ledgers, etc.), there might be different perspectives within the same country or region. So my aim is not to write an exhaustive overview of current regulation. Read this chapter only as an guideline to the existing regulation and certainly not as fixed truth!

© Stijn Van Hijfte 2020
S. Van Hijfte, *Decoding Blockchain for Business*,
https://doi.org/10.1007/978-1-4842-6137-8_4

Tax and Crypto Regulation in Europe

First of all, it might be easier to look into the Bitcoin network to start with. Why? It is simply the best known cryptocurrency by far, and has therefore caught the attention of regulators more than any of the other altcoins that currently exist.

If we take the case of the European Union, Bitcoin has legal status and conversion transactions are to this day not susceptible to VAT/GST, while transactions for goods and services are susceptible to income tax.[1] When it comes to the regulation of Bitcoin itself, there have been some confusing messages in the past. The European Central Bank stated in 2015 that financial sector regulation was not applicable to Bitcoin, as it did not involve traditional financial actors, while others stated that existing rules could be extended to Bitcoin and Bitcoin participants.[2,3] However, there is a move within Europe to increase the regulation on cryptocurrencies, introducing stricter rules, and this is based on the Anti-Money Laundering Directive (AMLD5) that has to be transposed into national law by each of the member states in January 2020.[4] There was also a ministerial resolution in 2016 that implemented a European Court of Justice decision. This decision stated that any transaction that involves the exchange of crypto-assets against fiat would not be tax deductible. This means that all crypto-transactions are liable to VAT.[5]

Looking at specific member states, we see that Germany forces asset exchanges and providers of crypto-payment and custodian services to apply for a license from the Federal Financial Supervisory Authority (Bafin). On top of that, cryptocurrencies are considered financial instruments. This provided a lot of clarity to people who want to participate in the market, but also raised the concern that this would send blockchain companies abroad or stop services (such as Bitpay).[6] Closely tied to Germany is the small nation of Liechtenstein, which has always had a favorable stance toward digital changes and similarly embraced the cryptocurrency world. On October 3, 2019, the Token and Trustworthy Technology Service Providers Act (TVTG) was approved.[7] With this new regulatory framework, Liechtenstein effectively became the first country in the world to regulate the token economy. The law uses the concept of the "Token Container Model," which states that "the

---

[1] www.loc.gov/law/help/bitcoin-survey/

[2] www.ecb.europa.eu/pub/pdf/other/virtualcurrencyschemes201210en.pdf

[3] www.europarl.europa.eu/RegData/bibliotheque/briefing/2014/140793/LDM_BRI(2014)140793_REV1_EN.pdf

[4] https://news.bitcoin.com/eu-members-adopt-tougher-crypto-rules-than-aml-directive-requires/

[5] https://unbank.mobi/cryptocurrency-regulation-italy/

[6] https://support.bitpay.com/hc/en-us/articles/360000123366-Why-can-t-I-use-BitPay-s-services-in-my-country-

[7] https://news.bitcoin.com/liechtenstein-adopts-token-act-to-attract-crypto-business/

token serves as a container for rights of all kinds, regardless whether it is stock, real estate, or license rights." This new regulation also sheds light on measures that need to be taken to prevent money laundering and terrorist financing. With this new framework, it aims to be one of the countries that can take on the crypto-economy and lure investors and companies to Liechtenstein. In Austria, there has been interesting news with the Ministry of Finance proposing a regulatory sandbox for the Fintech industry so that they can test their business models for a limited time under the supervision of the FMA.[8] It relates to the sandbox that has been developed by the Financial Conduct Authority in the UK. As with the other member states in the EU, the AMLD5 will be imposed in national law, but other than that, there has been no specific regulation of exchanges, miners, issuers, and sponsors.

Similarly, we see a trend toward stricter regulation in the Czech Republic regarding the crypto-industry. There is a requirement to apply for a license from the national trade licensing office, and failing to do so leads to massive fines.[9] Neighbor Slovakia has a dualistic view on cryptocurrencies: a means of exchange and an investment asset.[10] Profits are taxable for individuals under income tax (with costs relating to the activity deducted from the total amount), where the eventual tax rate is either 19% or 25% (depending on if it is lower or higher than 35,022.31 Euro). For businesses, cryptocurrencies are seen as short-term financial assets other than cash.

Estonia has traditionally been very open to the crypto-industry.[11] In the past there have been plans for a national cryptocoin (which were dropped), and the existing e-citizen program, which show the openness of Estonia for the crypto-industry and the innovation it brings. Cryptocurrencies have been classified as "value represented in digital form" and as in many other countries, these cryptocurrencies are seen as digital assets subject to tax purposes but not subject to VAT. With the AML/CFT act of 2017 and the new directive from the EU, regulations have a more robust boost to tighten control and the existing licensing scheme. Latvia has also started to recognize cryptocurrencies so that they are able to tax them. Together with Lithuania (and Estonia), they created a memorandum of understanding as early as 2017. The focus of this memorandum was broader than cryptocurrencies alone (the focus was the financial markets), but the fact that these were included shows that cryptocurrencies were seriously considered a part of the financial market.

---

[8]https://cointelegraph.com/news/austria-considers-establishment-of-fintech-regulatory-sandbox

[9]https://archiv.ihned.cz/c1-66620740-cesko-bude-opet-prisnejsi-nez-brusel-nova-regulace-kryptomen-dopadne-na-vetsi-okruh-firem-a-ohrozi-jejich-konkurenceschopnost

[10]https://medium.com/@blockpit/how-are-cryptocurrencies-regulated-in-slovakia-85b2e6e0bc18

[11]https://complyadvantage.com/knowledgebase/crypto-regulations/cryptocurrency-regulations-estonia/

The UK (despite at this date still dealing with Brexit discussions) still falls under the regulations that have been released by the EU. Even though there are no specific cryptocurrency laws as of yet, exchanges need to register with the Financial Conduct Authority and cryptocurrencies are not considered legal tender.[12] Investments in the crypto-industry here are subject to the capital gains tax and income tax, depending on the situation. With consultations with the crypto-industry within the UK now following, new regulations specific for the industry are on the horizon. This is clearing the way for detailed guidelines for participants and businesses.[13]

In France we also find the cryptocurrency world largely unregulated, with two ordinances on blockchain technology so far.[14] The first allowed the use of blockchain technology for a zero-coupon bond (minibon).[15] The second allowed further use of the technology for financial instruments.[16] There were also some warnings on the inherent risks of cryptocurrencies by the French Financial Market Authority (AMF) and the Prudential Supervisory Authority (ACPR), as Bitcoin and other cryptocurrencies don't fall under the financial instruments regulations of France.[17] Similarly in Belgium, the country issued a list of sources that should not be trusted when you consider the crypto-market.[18] When we consider the tax regulation in France, capital gains tax are in effect for gains from the sale of cryptocurrencies (there are different rules if this is occasional or professional) and these gains are included to calculate the wealth tax and gift tax. As with the other countries, more clarification is necessary in the future.

In Belgium, the FSMA imposed a ban on the marketing of products in which the return depends on virtual money to retail investors.[19] There have been several warnings in the past to warn the Belgian citizens about the possible dangers of investing in cryptocurrencies. Currently there is no body exercising prudential supervision and the deposit guarantee mechanism for bank accounts does not apply to virtual currency.[20] There are no plans to run a

---

[12]https://complyadvantage.com/knowledgebase/crypto-regulations/cryptocurrency-regulations-uk-united-kingdom/

[13]https://cointelegraph.com/news/uk-crypto-regulation-is-changing-recognition-looming-at-long-last

[14]www.loc.gov/law/help/cryptocurrency/france.php

[15]www.legifrance.gouv.fr/affichTexte.do?cidTexte=JORFTEXT000032465520and categorieLien=id

[16]www.legifrance.gouv.fr/affichTexte.do?cidTexte=JORFTEXT000036171908and categorieLien=id

[17]https://publications.banque-france.fr/sites/default/files/medias/documents/focus-10_2013-12-05_fr.pdf

[18]www.amf-france.org/en_US/Actualites/Communiques-de-presse/AMF/annee-2018?docId=workspace://SpacesStore/3f85fe88-fc1f-45b8-a55e-0bc5aeb298ce

[19]www2.deloitte.com/be/en/pages/financial-services/articles/fsi-regflash-cryptocurrencies.html

[20]https://medium.com/@blockpit/how-are-cryptocurrencies-regulated-in-belgium-b68ceaa809a0

Belgian regulatory framework, as the government and legislative bodies have called for more supervision and regulatory clarity at a European level so that this can be implemented in the country. The Netherlands, on the other hand, have unveiled measures to regulate providers of cryptocurrency services in an attempt to stop money laundering.[21] Providers need to officially register at the National Bank and have to submit themselves to a series of measures. In 2019, Luxembourg passed a bill to provide a legal framework concerning securities issued over the blockchain network. They would like to protect investors as well as reduce the number of intermediaries needed to perform transactions.[22]

Switzerland has a progressive stance toward cryptocurrencies and exchanges are legal. Cryptocurrencies are considered assets in the country by the Swiss Federal Tax Administration (SFTA).[23] These exchanges need to apply for a license and even ICOs are legal but have to comply to different rules depending on the situation.

In Italy, decree no. 90/2017 made regulations imposed on traditional money exchanges applicable to cryptocurrency exchanges. Profit and losses from cryptocurrency transactions are susceptible to corporate taxes. To this day, there are many uncertainties relating to taxation of cryptocurrencies. In the past, revenue from Bitcoin and other transactions were classified as profit from foreign exchange transactions, leading to a tax of 26%. The small state of San Marino approved a blockchain and cryptocurrency regulation in mid-2019, which should govern the topic and protect investors. They make a distinction between utility tokens, investment tokens, and cryptocurrencies, but also give tax exemptions in certain cases to businesses.[24]

In Spain there are very clear regulations in place to protect consumers and (retail) investors against possible cases of fraud. Cryptocurrencies cannot be treated as legal tender (only banknotes and coins denominated in Euros have legal tender status).[25] There was a warning on February 8, 2018 by the Spanish Securities and Exchange Commission (CNMV) and the bank of Spain warning investors not to invest in cryptocurrencies or ICOs. Depending on the situation, STOs (Security Token Offerings) might fall under the applicable regulations regarding the Spanish Stock Market Act (LMV). The only real regulation in the country so far relates to the taxation. Capital gains made from the sale of cryptocurrencies are taxed between 19% and 23%, unless the purchase and sale

[21]https://tech.newstatesman.com/fintech/netherlands-regulate-cryptocurrencies
[22]www.coindesk.com/luxembourg-passes-bill-to-give-blockchain-securities-legal-status
[23]https://complyadvantage.com/knowledgebase/crypto-regulations/cryptocurrency-regulations-switzerland/
[24]https://coinidol.com/san-marino-regulation/
[25]https://medium.com/@blockpit/how-are-cryptocurrencies-regulated-in-spain-e88a4cfc2b6a

took place within 12 months (24.75% to 52%). If the capital gains relate to a company, the tax is 25%. So far there has been no clear regulation on VAT.

Malta introduced an entire regulatory framework on November 1, 2018.[26] The goal is to protect investors as well as strengthen the existing cryptocurrency industry. There is a need for certification and companies wishing to perform an ICO to be in line with the regulations. Opposite of many other countries, the buying and selling of cryptocurrencies in Portugal is tax-free (ruling 5717/2015).[27] However, this does not apply to the exchange of cryptocurrencies for goods and services, and professional/businesses dealing in cryptocurrencies are still subject to some taxes. Portugal treats cryptocurrencies as a form of currency, which makes them exempt from VAT and capital gains taxes. This means that the country could become a bit of a tax heaven in the future if the crypto-industry really takes off in Europe.

Sweden has asked multiple times for clear regulatory guidelines when it comes to cryptocurrencies. While it is working on regulating the cryptocurrency space, it has also been researching the possibilities for a national cryptocurrency (e-krona).[28] This not to be confused with Kryptonex, which is a scam luring in people that were interested in the project.[29] The Swedish government has also auctioned off cryptocurrencies that had been taken from debtors to pay their debts.[30] So despite the fact that the country sometimes seems to take a staunch stance against cryptocurrencies, the authorities look to protect their citizens from the possible risks brought by these investments.

In Denmark, the Danish Tax Authority recently received the green light to collect user data from cryptocurrency exchanges to see if they have been paying their taxes.[31] There is also the Dansk Krypto Konsortium, which is a group of Danish blockchain companies that are working toward a regulatory framework in the country.[32] Norway has also enforced new money laundering regulations that apply to cryptocurrency exchanges and storage providers in the country.[33] Finanstilsynet (the Financial Supervisory Authority of Norway) also stated that firms storing private keys for customers are considered to be involved in the transfer, storage, or purchase of cryptocurrency. This means that providers have to register and comply with the newly imposed rules.

---

[26]www.aberdeen.com/techpro-essentials/blog-malta-becomes-the-first-country-to-regulate-cryptocurrency/

[27]www.forbes.com/sites/kellyphillipserb/2019/09/19/portugal-tax-authorities-clarify-that-buying-or-selling-cryptocurrency-is-tax-free/#5381f23477e3

[28]www.riksbank.se/en-gb/payments--cash/e-krona/

[29]https://blog.goodaudience.com/yes-sweden-is-launching-a-national-crypto-currency-but-its-not-kryptonex-2a730f7c3ac1

[30]https://news.bitcoin.com/swedish-government-auctions-cryptocurrency-again/

[31]www.coindesk.com/danish-tax-agency-to-collect-user-data-from-crypto-exchanges

[32]https://nordicblockchain.com/regulations/

[33]https://news.bitcoin.com/norway-crypto-service-providers/

Finland recently translated the EU anti-money laundering directive (AMLD5) into national regulation. The FIN-FSA stated that providers need to meet statutory requirements if they want to carry on their activities in the country.[34] Iceland had a more negative view of Bitcoin and cryptocurrencies in general as a consequence of the financial crisis of 2008.[35] Even though some major mining rigs can be found in the country, a release in 2013 stated that it was prohibited to engage in foreign exchange trading with Bitcoin. It meant in part that Bitcoin wasn't seen as a currency. Another attempt was made in 2014 with the launch of Auroracoin to step outside of the "Bitcoin restrictions" but because of the uncertainty regarding the regulations, the popularity of the coin remained below expectations.

In Poland, we can also see development in regulations. As of January 2019, revenues from cryptocurrency trading is either allocated as revenues from cash capital or revenues from investment income. The income from the sale of a virtual currency is taxed at 19%.[36] Miners will also have to pay income tax in the future on the profits they make with cryptocurrencies. Earlier, there had been warnings against the investment in virtual currency (similar to Spain) issued by the National Bank of Poland and the Financial Supervision Commission. Also similarly, cryptocurrencies are not recognized as legal tender.

Hungary is looking into regulating crypto-instruments and has set up a joint workgroup that consists of the central bank, the tax authority, and the finance ministry (and other authorities) looking into the legal, economic, and law enforcement issues relating to cryptocurrencies.[37] Currently, it has a very unfavorable personal income tax framework that imposes 15% personal income tax and 22% health contribution. There are often extra administrative requirements and there have been many new investment schemes that leave the investor unprotected or leading up to even more taxes.

Next on the list is Romania, which taxed the income from cryptocurrencies. Depending on the value (lower than 200 RON isn't taxed, higher than 600 RON a year leads to 10% income tax), other taxation percentages are in place.[38] There is also a draft in place that focuses on the regulation of electronic money (emergency ordinance published by the Ministry of Finance).[39] This regulation would task the Romanian National Bank with the oversight of the issuing entities and would impose certain requirements on them. As with

---

[34]https://thenextweb.com/hardfork/2019/04/29/finlands-new-cryptocurrency-regulation-forces-aml-on-industry/
[35]www.thebalance.com/iceland-time-to-free-bitcoin-4030896
[36]https://medium.com/altcoin-magazine/how-are-cryptocurrencies-regulated-in-poland-c8e590e078ec
[37]https://bitcoinist.com/hungary-not-consider-cryptocurrency-legal-tender/
[38]https://news.bitcoin.com/romania-imposes-10-tax-on-cryptocurrency-earnings/
[39]https://news.bitcoin.com/draft-regulating-electronic-money-prepared-in-romania/

many other European countries, there have been several warnings to not invest in cryptocurrencies, as they carry within them clear risks.

Bulgaria has a more positive outlook on cryptocurrencies, as it was the first nation state to have more Bitcoin holdings than gold reserves.[40] Their current holdings are believed to surpass 213,000 Bitcoins. However, so far there has been no clear development of a framework within the country. There are also no license requirements as of yet when it comes to the business use of cryptocurrencies.[41] Today, the profits from cryptocurrency trading are subject to 10% tax.

Greece has seen a total of 31 companies working as cryptocurrency exchanges. The reason that there have been so many cryptocurrency exchanges in the country, and why there is an overall popularity of cryptocurrencies, relates back to the financial crisis of 2009 and the impact on the economy.[42]

So far there are no mechanisms for legal protection in place when we look at the Republic of Serbia. This means that people who wish to engage in the cryptocurrency industry bear all the risk for these activities.[43] There is the law on the National Bank of Serbia, which involves the licensing of payment institutions, including licenses for issuing electronic money to e-money institutions. This does not include licenses for cryptocurrencies trading! Similarly, Montenegro and Bosnia-Herzegovina do not seem to have any legal framework on the topic. Albania has a more innovative view of blockchain technology, as they opened up public consultations for a legislative act on the financial market by using a blockchain framework. This way they try to become more democratic, open, and transparent when it comes to the legislative process in their country. The National Bank of Macedonia, on the other hand, issued a warning against cryptocurrencies as according to local regulation, foreign bank accounts or securities aren't allowed (there are certain exceptions).[44] In Croatia, both the National bank and the Financial Stability Council issued warnings because of the possible losses and taxation of cryptocurrency investments. In the same vein, the Bank of Slovenia also issued a warning on the topic.

Belarus has the Presidential Decree on the development of the digital economy, which regulates the issuance and use of cryptocurrencies and tokens.[45] Many of the regulations in the decree extend to legal entities operating on the territory of the high technologies park (which is a special

---

[40]www.trustnodes.com/2019/07/21/bulgarias-bitcoin-holdings-surpass-their-gold-reserves

[41]www.nomoretax.eu/bulgaria-crypto-owner/

[42]https://cryptobit.media/en/news/other/1306/

[43]https://nebojsa.com/blog/legislation-on-cryptocurrency-business-operations-in-serbia.html

[44]www.loc.gov/law/help/cryptocurrency/world-survey.php

[45]www.loc.gov/law/help/cryptocurrency/belarus.php

economic zone in the country). Any actions with cryptocurrencies (including mining) are allowed in the country as a natural person, as long as you do it alone, and as long as you don't use it to buy goods and services. There are also clear licensing requirements, foreign exchange controls, and reporting requirements, making it one of the countries with the most comprehensive and clear frameworks in place for the cryptocurrency industry.

In Russia, there has been more attention toward the use and possibilities of cryptocurrencies compared to many other countries. In 2019 a new digital rights act was released that defines smart contracts and cryptocurrency tokens.[46] Specifically, this bill focuses on the legal impact of these concepts and how legal rights can be transferred. On top of that, there has been a new regulation adoption that classifies crypto-assets under three separate legal categories: virtual assets, technical tokens, and digital finance assets.[47] Bitcoin can be seen as a virtual asset (store of value), Ether as a technical token (as you need it to release functions on the Ethereum blockchain), and ICOs fall under the last category.

A land with a lot of political and economic turmoil in recent years is Ukraine. Because of this there has been no real focus on cryptocurrencies. So far the only accepted currencies in the country are the national currency (hryvnia) and foreign currencies released by a central authority.[48] This does not mean that there is no work being done on the subject, as there have recently been two drafts released on the subject. As long as there is no official regulation on cryptocurrencies, they are subject to standard income tax (18% for individuals, for businesses it depends on their line of business). If the two drafts are accepted, there will be a favorable regulatory framework in the country, as crypto-transactions would drop to a tax rate of 5% for individuals. After 2024, businesses would have to pay 18%. The second draft focuses on consumer protection, supervision, and a clear legal framework. There is also a draft that wants to exempt crypto-transactions from tax altogether until 2030. The national bank of Moldova issued a warning in 2018 on crypto-assets because of the nature of the vehicle and the absence of clear regulations. Transnistria, on the other hand, passed a law legalizing mining activities.

Finally, there is Turkey. Cryptocurrencies have an enormous popularity there. Depending on the source, at least 20% of the population owns tokens. In its 11th Development Plan, 2019-2023, Turkey also proposed the formation of a blockchain-based central bank money.[49] While real regulation is still at a minimum, there have even been drafts of something called a "Turkcoin".

---

[46]https://thenextweb.com/hardfork/2019/10/02/russia-reportedly-enacts-laws-cryptocurrency-smart-contracts/
[47]https://coinrivet.com/russia-cryptocurrency-regulation/
[48]https://medium.com/@blockpit/how-are-cryptocurrencies-regulated-in-ukraine-afc5d24a8c0f
[49]www.dailysabah.com/op-ed/2019/08/20/turkish-law-on-blockchain-tech

Tax and Crypto Regulation in Asia

Depending on the topic, you can see that adoption of cryptocurrencies is happening faster in Asia than anywhere else in the world. You have to keep in mind that each country has its own view and approach to the topic.

One country that has made considerable efforts on the topic is Singapore, where the Monetary Authority of Singapore wishes to refrain from regulating cryptocurrencies. The goal is to create a regulatory framework surrounding cryptocurrencies rather than regulating the cryptocurrencies themselves. However, there is a possibility for double taxation in the case of Bitcoin, where there is a tax on purchase and when using it to purchase a good or service.[50] As one of the major blockchain hubs of Asia and the world, keeping the regulations as open as possible seems to be one of the goals of the country.

Chinese regulators have also responded to the rise of blockchain technology. China isn't really embracing the technology as you would expect in other countries but rather is using certain parts to their benefit.[51] Major companies such as Alibaba and Tencent have been working on implementations of the technology to improve their way of working. So what is different here compared to the rest of the world? According to new regulation, "entities" providing "blockchain information services" need to register with the government and collect information about the users, thereby actively undermining some of the fundamental concepts that formed the start of blockchain in the first place. For the Chinese government, it can prove to be a tool to gain further control over its citizens when it comes to digital information, identity, and transactions.

The Indian government has started with the creation of a regulatory framework for blockchain technology. The potential of the technology and the need for infrastructure demand the setup of such a framework.[52] One use case that was implemented in India is the pilot of a blockchain system for property registration at the Shamshabad District and the KYC solution developed at Telangana state. The use of cryptocurrency is another story as the use of such tokens can lead to fines and jail time (based on proposed sanctions). So while half the states in India have started projects with blockchain technology, the very concept of cryptocurrencies is banned by the central bank.[53] However, the topic is still very contentious and the stance of India and their central bank might change over time (also due to pressure of the public).

---

[50]www.asiablockchainreview.com/singapore-blockchain-regulations-and-landscape/

[51]www.technologyreview.com/f/614639/chinas-leaders-have-embraced-blockchains-erm-minus-the-decentralized-bit/

[52]www.asiatimes.com/2019/11/article/blockchain-india-working-on-regulatory-framework/

[53]https://forkast.news/india-regulation-cryptocurrency-blockchain-ownership-ban-analysis/

Another leading blockchain adopter is Japan. It has shown to be more than willing to adopt the technology.[54] An important reason for the level of adoption in Japan is the stance of the government. Where many governments saw a possible disruptor, Japan saw a technology that can enhance existing processes and infrastructure. The regulation has been set up in such a way that the blockchain industry is further boosted while its citizens are protected from possible mishaps. There are clear regulations on cryptocurrencies: what cryptocurrencies are, sales tokens, how are they taxed, and what the AML regulations are. This created certainty for companies wanting to move forward in their adoption of distributed ledgers.

An example where a country has taken a very negative stance toward cryptocurrencies is Vietnam, where the use of cryptocurrencies as a means of payment is strictly banned and forbidden. At the same time any other regulatory framework for crypto-assets is still lacking.

Cambodia has taken a similar stance without a clear regulatory scheme, while a statement was released by the Exchange Commission of Cambodia, the National Bank of Cambodia, and the General-Commissariat of the National Police that stated that if regulation would be created, they would be involved. Without a license, buying, selling, trading, or propagation and settlement are all deemed illegal. However, to this day, there is no licensing scheme in place, which means developing cryptocurrencies in the country is still illegal.[55]

Laos has released two notifications and a warning regarding cryptocurrencies. Notification No. 314/BOL encourages the population of the country to be more knowledgeable of cryptocurrencies. The same notification clearly stated that there is no regulatory framework in place and that the population cannot use cryptocurrencies as money or use it to pay debts. Notification No. 382/BOL also prohibited financial institutions from engaging in cryptocurrency-related activities.

Indonesia prohibited crypto-assets as early as 2018, but by the end of the year, the Ministry of Trade released Regulation No. 99, officially classifying cryptocurrencies as commodities.[56] The Commodity Futures Trading Regulatory Agency or BAPPEBTI is the main regulator involved in the supervision of crypto-assets trading in the country. Regulations No. 5 and 9 helped legalize the sale and purchase of crypto-assets. Other involved institutions are the Indonesian Financial Transaction Reports and Analysis Center (PPATK), which focuses on anti-money laundering, and the Bank of Indonesia.

---

[54]https://hackernoon.com/japan-is-fast-becoming-the-gold-standard-for-blockchain-adoption-p3s32kni
[55]www.lexology.com/library/detail.aspx?g=33dabdac-5ee5-4fb3-af6f-9d7ea38b340f
[56]www.asiablockchainreview.com/blockchain-regulation-and-landscape-in-indonesia/

Being the world leader in Internet access speed, with a population that has over 92% of the Internet users, blockchain clearly shows potential in South Korea.[57] However, due to the many abuses of ICOs in recent years, the government has issued a ban on them since 2017. In the same vein that cryptocurrencies are sometimes seen as a threat to the national economy. A "regulation-free" zone was created in Busan, where some of the restrictions are dropped so that experimentation becomes possible in certain cases.

Myanmar has only published one official statement on cryptocurrencies, authored by the Central Bank of Myanmar. It stated that the CBM is the only institution issuing and managing a domestic currency. Cryptocurrencies are therefore not recognized as a means of payment in the country. In the same vein, financial institutions are prohibited from buying, selling, or exchanging cryptocurrencies.

Thailand is currently the leader in Southeast Asia when it comes to the creation of a clear regulatory framework regarding cryptocurrencies. The 2018 Emergency Decree on Digital Asset Businesses helps regulate all cryptocurrency-related activities. Digital assets are considered goods and are subject to 7% VAT and capital gains from the sale of digital assets are subject to income tax. Clear requirements have been set for ICO portals (electronic system provider) and digital asset businesses.

When we look at the Middle East, we see some differences, as some countries are taking more action than others. Saudi Arabia, Bahrain, and Lebanon have showed key interest in blockchain technology and are leading the charge in the region. The main difference compared to the other regions and countries is that adoption of blockchain solutions is mainly driven from the top down.[58] Examples are the launch of a digital currency by Saudi Arabia and the UAE, called "Aber," and would help facilitate financial settlements between the two nations, and the emCash currency of Dubai. Because of these developments, regulation is a hot topic as well. The UAE has taken steps to warn investors about the risks involved with cryptocurrencies and at the same time provide a regulatory framework that recognizes digital tokens as securities. A second example is Abu Dhabi, where the financial regulator granted approval for Arabian Bourse so that a full-fledged crypto-asset exchange and digital custodian can operate. Other countries in the region are quickly following, such as Saudi Arabia, Egypt, and Kuwait, where regulators have started to design frameworks considering cryptocurrencies and moving away from their previous stance (earlier cryptocurrencies were considered not Sharia-compliant).

---

[57]https://thediplomat.com/2019/11/what-hides-behind-south-korean-cryptocurrency-regulation-policy/

[58]www.financemagnates.com/cryptocurrency/regulation/cryptocurrency-in-arab-world-clock-is-ticking-but-pace-to-remain-slow/

Tax and Crypto Regulation in Africa

Depending on the source, up to 35% of Africa's population doesn't have access to financial services. Blockchain technology might help in this regard and give these people access.[59]

As mobile telecommunication usage also made a huge leap forward from 3% to over 80% in a decade, the use of local mobile and e-payment platforms has become generally accepted. However, in general, the continent doesn't seem to be really busy with creating regulations on the topic. One of the exceptions is South Africa, where new regulations have been created to govern the use of cryptocurrencies.[60] Similar to the local currency, these regulations also limit the amount that can be sent outside of the country. In even more recent months, over 30 recommendations for further regulation of cryptocurrencies have been made.[61] All activities will be closely monitored to protect the population while at the same time, crypto-assets cannot be considered electronic money.

In Kenya, there are also serious considerations for blockchain regulation as it is seen by some as the technology of the future.[62] The technology is seen as a possible solution to prevent corruption and make the country one of the new leaders of the future when it comes to innovation and economic growth. In that sense, Kenya is becoming a leader in blockchain adoption across the continent.

Nigeria is also trying to become more digital and there has been the launch of a passenger manifest system on top of a blockchain platform for traveling by road. As the infrastructure in the country isn't top notch, traveling by road is the main way of transportation, and insurance for these kinds of travel can now be bought on a blockchain solution. As kidnappings are rampant in certain cases and authorities struggle to find the next of kin (with paper-based manifests that are far from complete), this solution should aid in protecting citizens.

Ghana has slowly started looking into regulation for cryptocurrencies even though the central bank has plans to release a digital currency in 2020 (it seems unlikely that this will be a blockchain-based currency).[63] All it has done

[59]www.dailymaverick.co.za/article/2019-04-08-blockchain-and-cryptocurrency-regulation-in-africa/

[60]https://thenextweb.com/hardfork/2019/12/03/south-africa-central-bank-cryptocurrency-rules-bitcoin-regulation/

[61]https://news.bitcoin.com/south-africa-cryptocurrency/

[62]https://cointelegraph.com/news/africa-using-blockchain-to-drive-change-nigeria-and-kenya-part-one

[63]https://cointelegraph.com/news/ghana-joins-the-bandwagon-plans-for-cbdc-still-wary-of-crypto

so far is issue a public warning to investors in March 2019. In this warning it states that investors should do their due diligence and at the same time they included 24 cryptocurrencies that have gained prominence worldwide.

Similar to Ghana, the Democratic Republic of Congo still has no formal regulation in place when it comes to cryptocurrencies. Other countries that still have no regulation in place are Angola, Benin, Botswana, Burkina Faso, Burundi, Cameroon, Cape Verde, Central African Republic, Chad, Comoros, Côte d'Ivoire, Djibouti, and many others.

Algeria has come down extremely hard on cryptocurrencies and has prohibited the purchase, sale, use, and possession of cryptocurrencies since 2018.

The central bank of Eswatini has issued a statement that cryptocurrencies are not enjoying legal-tender status and aren't regulated. Therefore it wanted to warn the population about the use of cryptocurrencies.[64]

Lesotho's central bank warned the public as well for the use of cryptocurrencies and officially stated that they do not oversee any of these. It isn't regarded as legal tender or foreign currency so people engaging in trading do so at their own risk. Central banks in several other countries have issued warnings as well, such as Uganda and Zimbabwe.

Tax and Crypto Regulation in Oceania

In Australia, just as in many other countries, the use of cryptocurrencies is in a legal gray area.[65] You can hold them without any problem but spending them is not possible. According to their regulations, actually spending cryptocurrency is an illegal operation. However, the country has been moving to more open regulations and has removed the previous double taxation of Bitcoin.[66] New regulations are being considered for exchanges as well as for the identification (KYC/AML) of those performing transactions. As the government becomes more and more familiar with the technology, one can suspect clearer regulations for enterprises that want to enter the market.

In New Zealand it has become legal to pay employees in Bitcoin.[67] Whether this is a good or a bad idea, it clearly shows the intentions of the government and its vision of cryptocurrencies. Believing in the technology and its use as a

---

[64]https://trading-education.com/cryptocurrency-regulation-around-the-world-in-2019-ranked#:~:text=In%20the%20Democratic%20Republic%20of,which%20is%20a%20good%20sign.

[65]www.asiablockchainreview.com/blockchain-regulation-in-australia/

[66]https://complyadvantage.com/knowledgebase/crypto-regulations/cryptocurrency-regulations-australia/

[67]https://thenextweb.com/hardfork/2019/08/12/new-zealand-bitcoin-salary-regulation-bad-idea/

form of payment, they have taken a progressive stance toward cryptocurrencies and blockchain as a whole.[68]

The Marshall Islands is dealing with a gray area when it comes to cryptocurrency regulations, while it is creating its own cryptocurrency at the same time, called SOV. It will be tied to the US dollar and will be used for debts, public charges, taxes, and dues.

Tax and Crypto Regulation in the Americas

Finally, there are the Americas. As we have seen and one might suspect, everything depends on the country when we talk about regulations. In Canada, for example, there is still regulatory uncertainty when it comes to blockchain and cryptocurrencies.[69] Currently the regulation is seen as ambiguous, so it isn't clear what is possible and what isn't. This uncertainty is hurting their economy, as numerous companies within the country are actually considering investments in the technology.

The United States is also struggling with regulation. As of the end of 2019, there are 21 bills in congress concerning blockchain technology.[70] One of these bills focuses on the possible negative impact of cryptocurrencies, such as tax evasion, terrorism, and human trafficking and how one could possibly track such tokens. A second bill focuses on how companies can use cryptocurrencies in their current business models, while a third goes in-depth on how the government might use the technology in the future. The fact that the United States already had a robust and strict framework relating to financial services might also have a major impact on how blockchain is perceived in the country.[71]

So while being a lead innovator of the Western world, there have been delays in adoption, as the country struggles to find a balance between its regulations while promoting business as well as protecting its citizens. It has to be said that the United States is the most important country when it comes to cryptocurrencies and its approach to regulating cryptocurrencies will probably influence its allies. Cryptocurrencies are considered a property and not a currency in the country, so specific taxes are applicable. Another important

---

[68]www.americanbanker.com/opinion/new-zealands-progressive-approach-is-a-boost-for-cryptocurrency

[69]https://tokenpost.com/Canadas-regulatory-uncertainty-on-blockchain-stunts-exponential-growth-Canadian-Digital-Chamber-of-Commerce-report-3771

[70]www.forbes.com/sites/jasonbrett/2019/12/21/crypto-legislation-2020-analysis-of-21-cryptocurrency-and-blockchain-bills-in-congress/#3927c83656c1

[71]https://cointelegraph.com/news/why-is-the-us-not-yet-a-leader-in-crypto-regulation-experts-answer

aspect is that there might be important differences within states, such as the BitLicense in New York.

In Latin America, Bolivia has issued harsh regulations, as cryptocurrencies and exchanges are simply banned all together.[72]

Anguilla introduced some regulations, most focusing on the release of ICOs while some consider securities regulated by existing regulation. At the same time, it is part of the ECCB (Eastern Caribbean Central Bank) pilot where a cryptocurrency is tested alongside the national currency. Antigua and Barbuda are also part of the ECCB's pilot and at the same time the government has supported the development of the Antigua and Barbuda Development coin, even though it isn't state sponsored.

In the Bahamas, the government is looking into blockchain technology to simplify transactions. Similarly, they are looking into the use of a digital version of the national Bahamian dollar. However, the government is also preparing regulation that should help prevent the use of cryptocurrencies for money laundering or terrorist financing. Barbados is also looking into creating its own cryptocurrency, which would be tied to the Barbadian dollar through a company called "Bitt inc".

Ecuador, on the other hand, has chosen to ban all cryptocurrencies except for the national government-issued SDE-token. Countries such as Mexico, Argentina, Brazil, Venezuela, and Chile have accepted cryptocurrencies as a form of payment. Mexico did update its anti-money laundering regulation to include cryptocurrencies and companies offering cryptocurrency-related services.

Costa Rica has considered cryptocurrencies legal even though it is not considered legal tender or foreign currency. Some warnings have been released by the central bank, while it has also stated that it is not looking into regulating or supervising cryptocurrencies for payments.

In the case of Venezuela, cryptocurrencies offer an escape from the freefall of the Bolívar and the economic crisis.[73] It has also created its own cryptocurrency, called the Petro, which is backed by the value of Venezuelan oil.

The "Cripto InterCambio" exchange of Chile wants to further open the Latin American world to blockchain technology and vows to invest in startups that wish to explore the topic.[74]

---

[72]https://complyadvantage.com/knowledgebase/crypto-regulations/cryptocurrency-regulations-latin-america/

[73]www.visualcapitalist.com/mapped-cryptocurrency-regulations-around-the-world/

[74]https://cointelegraph.com/news/exchange-vows-to-offer-easy-access-to-crypto-for-latin-america

GDPR and Blockchain

When you discuss the possibilities of blockchain, you will eventually run into discussions regarding GDPR (General Data Protection Regulation) in Europe. The GDPR has been quite recently imposed within the EU and can lead to huge fines if people or businesses are found to be non-compliant. Blockchain poses a bit of an issue when you consider several elements of the regulatory framework. Please consider the fact that I don't discuss all regulatory specifications, but only want to provide an overview of possible contention with the GDPR regulation. This means that there are more possible areas of conflict between blockchain technology and GDPR, but also that I didn't list all measures and stipulations defined within the GDPR regulation. This would require a completely different book and is certainly reason for future research.

The first factor that might form an issue is the underlying assumption of the GDPR framework. There is at least one natural or legal person one can address (the data controller) to enforce personal rights considering the personal data that is being processed. With blockchains we are dealing with a decentralized technology that seeks, more often than not, decentralized consensus. Without a clear person or group of persons in place, it is difficult, if not impossible, to determine who is responsible or accountable.[75] There is the concept of "joint-controllership" in the regulation, which makes it even more difficult, as you could consider all miners working toward consensus responsible and accountable for the personal data being processed. This can only be determined on a case-by-case basis where the governance design of the blockchain use case must be examined to identify the actors that determine the purpose and means of data processing.

This also means that parties that exercise influence over the software, hardware, and datacenters that process data for the blockchain application can be considered to have influence over the data processing as a whole. Similarly, the purpose of the blockchain application can be influenced by many factors and actors, so that the determination of (joint) controllership can be a difficult task. Even when you use a private blockchain, and a legal entity is created for the consortium participating in the network, all separate entities taking part in the consortium could possibly be considered joint controllers.

For public blockchains we have to look at several participants. There are the software developers, but they generally do not determine whether an update is accepted, so they are rarely identified as controllers. Similarly, it seems unlikely that miners will be identified as controllers, as they have no influence over the purpose or means of processing. It has been suggested that the nodes in the network could be considered controllers so far that these nodes initiate

---

[75]www.europarl.europa.eu/RegData/etudes/STUD/2019/634445/EPRS_STU(2019) 634445_EN.pdf

transactions (distributing data through the network) or save transaction data in its own copy of the database.[76] Others have suggested that a combination of miners and nodes could be considered the joint controllers of a public blockchain network.[77] Finally, there are the users, the participants in the network, which could be considered controllers of the transactions they submit. A recent European Parliament report embraces the same view in suggesting that users "may be both data controllers, for the personal data that they upload to the ledger, and data processors, by virtue of storing a full copy of the ledger on their own computer".[78] On top of that, recent cases have shown that the qualifying factors to define the entities responsible are fraught with a lack of certainty. You should also consider that even when you can determine the controller of joint controllers in a specific case, this controller might be unable to comply with the GDPR regulation, as they simply have no control over the data and the application as a whole. There is also the possibility for certain participants in the network to be identified as a processor instead of being a controller. Although processors have fewer responsibilities than controllers, that doesn't mean that there are none. They must follow the instructions of the controller, allow supervision from the controller to make sure all the right actions are taken, maintain a record of all processing activities they carry out for the controller, provide a general description of the technical and organizational security measures, and in some cases appoint a data protection officer. They also have to provide records to the data protection authority on request and, in the case of a data breach, the processor must alert the controller without undue delay after becoming aware of the breach.[79] Depending on the situation, software developers could be considered data processors based on the role they assume in the project.[80] This division between processors and controllers leads to other issues and uncertainties as the GDPR regulation requires a legal act between processors and controllers. It is not the determining factor, so if there is a later decision that this relationship does exist in a specific context, this legal relationship can be created a posteriori.

Secondly, there is the assumption in GDPR that data can be modified or erased where necessary to comply with legal requirements. This seems antithetical to blockchain technology when you consider that blockchains' integrity mechanism is built on the fact that data can not be unilaterally

---

[76]Martini M and Weinzierl Q (2017), "Die Blockchain-Technologie und das Recht auf Vergessenwerden," 17 *Neue Zeitschrift für Verwaltungsrecht* 1251, 1253

[77]Bacon J et al (2018) "Blockchain Demystified: A Technical and Legal Introduction to Distributed and Centralised Ledgers," 25 *Richmond Journal of Law and Technology* 1, 71-72

[78]European Parliament (27 November 2018), *Report on Blockchain: a Forward-Looking Trade Policy* (AB-0407/2018) para 22

[79]Article 33(2) GDPR

[80]Commission Nationale Informatique et Libertés (September 2018), *Premiers Éléments d'analyse de la CNIL: Blockchain,* 2 www.cnil.fr/sites/default/files/atoms/files/la_blockchain.pdf

modified within the chain, let alone erased. One could argue that hashed data or public keys stored on the public ledger are no longer considered personal data but within the scope of GDPR this is certainly not the case. You can immediately link this to the question of whether data can be anonymized enough to qualify for GDPR compliance. One of the requirements in the GDPR is that of accuracy, which mandates that person data should be accurate and, where necessary, kept up to date.[81] This also relates to the right of modification, which can lead to issues when you consider the nature of blockchain applications.[82] There is a division we should make between private/permissioned blockchain applications that can more easily comply with these rules and public/permissionless blockchains. Most discussions, however, relate to the right of erasure stipulated in the GDPR.[83] This right of erasure is not an absolute right, but rather a qualified and a limited right and must be balanced against the considerations in Article 17(2) GDPR. Even though most people think they have a clear knowledge of what "erasure" means, there is no clear definition of this in the regulation, leaving it open to interpretation. Recent court cases have shown that it doesn't necessarily mean that the data is destroyed, but rather that data controllers have to take the necessary actions within their control to secure the result as close as possible to the destruction of their data within their own possibilities. However, there seems to be still some differences in interpretation within the different member states of the EU, so that only future case law can hopefully provide a clear definition.

As you can clearly see here, and also further in these pages, a lot is still open to interpretation and it will be up to the regulatory bodies to give guidance about practical implementations of this and other regulations. Otherwise, these might prove to be a hindrance to innovation and future growth within the borders of the EU. One way of looking at this specific issue is by considering the governance framework in place of a particular blockchain application. Article 29 working party considered cloud technology and stated that personal data can only be considered "erased" if all copies existing on redundant hardware are also erased. When we look at the blockchain network, this means that personal data has to be erased from each of the nodes. This also means that if a subject wants to enforce his right of erasure at a data controller, this controller must initiate erasure from other controllers/processors. There have been writers who take the analogy from the Google Spain ECJ case[84] and imagine that data subjects might contact block explorers

---

[81] Article 5(1)(d) GDPR

[82] Article 26 GDPR

[83] Article 17 GDPR

[84] Case C-131/12 Google Spain [2014] EU:C:2014:317, para 80. The Court emphasized that search engines made it easier for Internet users to find the relevant data and played an important role in its dissemination, which was "liable to constitute a more significant interference with the data subject's fundamental right to privacy than the publication on the web page."

from removing their personal data from these explorers instead of from the actual underlying infrastructure.[85] Within the scope of personal data, distributed ledger technology and GDPR, we also have to look into the stipulations that define the transfer of personal data to third countries. When we look into the regulation, data can be transferred to third countries if this is the result of an adequacy decision, appropriate safeguards are offered, or it's on the basis of a derogation.[86] When the data transfer takes place, the data subject must be informed of this. You can see that blockchain technology can both offer solutions (data subjects can follow where their personal data has traveled) and problems (how do you stop your personal data from being processed in third countries when you consider public/permissionless blockchains).

Linked to these points, we have the communication duties of the data controller in regards to the data subjects.[87] In private distributed ledger setups, this shouldn't prove any issue, as you can clearly track who had access to someone's personal data, while in public/permissionless blockchain setups this is impossible, leading to non-compliance with the GDPR regulation.

When you look at these two clear points of tension between GDPR and blockchain technology, one should always keep this in mind when designing blockchain solutions. IT architects need to be aware of these concepts and have to design their solutions and the governance systems surrounding them in such a way to prevent contention as much as possible. But we also have to consider the legal uncertainties surrounding GDPR considering blockchain technology but also other digital innovations. Only the future will be able to show us how the regulation can be brought to terms with these new developments.

There are also some other point of possible contention. One of these relates to article 3 GDPR which relates to when GDPR can be applied. This relates to the establishment of a controller or a processor in the European Union regardless of whether the processing itself takes place in the EU or not.[88] Based on previous cases before the European Court of Justice, establishment is based on concepts such as "the degree of stability of the arrangements and the effective exercise of activities which must be interpreted in the light of the specific nature of the economic activities and the provision of services concerned".[89] Based on this, we can see that a functional approach trumps formal analysis. More importantly, the GDPR regulation applies if the personal data being processed relates to data subject that are based in the EU, even

---

[85]www.europarl.europa.eu/RegData/etudes/STUD/2019/634445/EPRS_STU(2019)634445_EN.pdf

[86]Article 45 – 46 GDPR

[87]Article 19 GDPR

[88]https://eur-lex.europa.eu/legal-content/NL/TXT/?uri=CELEX%3A32016R0679

[89]https://eur-lex.europa.eu/legal-content/NL/TXT/?uri=CELEX%3A62014CJ0230

when the data controller / processor are not established in the EU (when one of two conditions are met).[90] A first condition applies to when personal data is being processed when goods and services are offered, irrespective of whether a payment of the data subject is required. A second possibility applies to data processing in the context of monitoring of behavior when this behavior takes place within the EU. A third (not very common) possibility relates to the processing of personal data in the scope of public international law. When you follow these definitions, you can clearly see that there are many instances when the GDPR will apply, whether or not you are working with blockchain technology. The main "Data Protection Authority" or "DPA" (each member state has one), that is responsible for the entity processing the data, this can offer a difficult question. For private/permissioned blockchain technology, the competent DPA will be most likely the one of the main establishment of the data controller. For public/permissionless blockchain platforms, this can be more of an issue. Probably there will be again a functional approach where "the main establishment" cannot be established so that the analysis will focus on the relevant activities for the processing and where they were carried out.[91] Also those that think that they can escape the GDPR because they are not "really" processing data are out of luck. Processing of personal data is being defined as "any operation or set of operations which is performed on personal data or sets of personal data".[92] This means that any handling of personal data qualifies as processing (including the storage of data). There is however, an important exemption from this general consideration called the "household exemption". This exemption states that the GDPR regulation does not apply to the processing of personal data by a natural person that occurs in the course of purely personal or household activity where it has no connection to a professional or commercial activity. The French Commission Nationale de l'Informatique et des Libertés (CNIL) announced in 2018, in its guideline on blockchains, that some cases may fall under this exception. One of the examples given was the buying and selling of Bitcoin from one person their own account. Whether the ECJ will take the same approach is to be seen, as they deem that the household exceptions needs to be interpreted strictly. According to that same ECJ, the household exemption cannot be applied in those cases where the processing activity is carried out in the course of private or family life of individuals while at the same time it is made accessible to an indefinite number of people. Hello, blockchain! Based on this you can understand that it is questionable if the household exemption can ever be applied to personal data processing through blockchain.

We will not go into all the details on how personal data is defined within the GDPR regulation but for one to understand it, the regulation takes a very

---

[90]Article 3(2) GDPR
[91]http://curia.europa.eu/juris/liste.jsf?language=nlandnum=C-131/12
[92]Article 4(2) GDPR

broad approach to what might be classified as personal data, including and not limited to: public keys, internet protocol addresses, cookie identifiers, radio frequency identification tags and more. Recital 26 GDPR recalls that pseudonymous data is qualified as personal data in line with article 4(5) GDPR. However, this recital introduces a test to see whether the data can still be considered personal data or not. If the controller or another person are able to identify the data subject in using all the means reasonably to be used, it is still considered personal data, and otherwise it is no longer personal data.[93] This recital takes a risk-based approach, while the original Article 29 working party had a more zero-risk approach as it defined anonymization as "irreversibly prevent identification". Which line will be followed in the long term can only be seen over time and is currently reason for uncertainty. The recital 26 takes also technical developments into consideration but it is very from clear which timescales should be taken into consideration. You could think about the possible impact of quantum computing on blockchain technology and the existing encryption standards as a whole.

Transactional data is another concept specific to blockchain technology which may be identified as personal data. When we refer back to the CNIL, this is all data contained within a transaction (can be anything from diploma, property deed, name, address, …). As you can see this really needs to be analyzed on a case by case basis to determine when we are dealing with personal data or data that cannot be covered with this term. As long as the data being transacted can be used to directly or indirectly identify a natural person, we are dealing with personal data. When we only consider financial data, we have to take into account the "motivated-intruder test" which has been used in the past in the UK. This test requires organizations to consider whether individuals could be re-identified from the anonymized data by someone who is reasonably competent, has access to resources such as the internet and would employ investigative techniques, such as making enquiries of people who may have additional knowledge of the identity of the data subject. The motivated intruder is not assumed to have any specialist knowledge.[94] This means that you cannot simply state that financial transaction data is not personal data as in the past it has been proven that people could be identified based on their transactional data (there have been examples in the past in the Bitcoin network).[95]

With all these examples, we also have to consider the off-chain database that is linked to the blockchain based application. This could be a solution to the discussions surrounding the personal data that has been stored in the actual chain transactions. When you keep the personal data in an off-chain database,

---

[93]Recital 26 GDPR
[94]https://itlaw.wikia.org/wiki/Motivated-intruder_test#cite_note-0
[95]www.researchgate.net/publication/277248535_Identifying_Bitcoin_users_by_transaction_behavior

this data could be dealt with in a much easier fashion. The data within the transactions themselves could only contain information to access the personal data in this separate database.[96] Another possibility that might help in the discussions surrounding personal data and blockchain applications is the use of zero-knowledge proofs which deliver the proof without sharing the actual data to do so. This could solve issues relating to data minimization and data verifiability between several partners.[97] A third strategy to reduce the likelihood of identification is the use of stealth addresses which are addresses that are generated to be used only for a one-time transaction and relies on hashed one-time keys. By using this technology, you could consider the "motivated-intruder" test, where it is nearly impossible to identify the participants as you cannot simply link transactions together to identify natural persons. A fourth technology that can be used to achieve "anonymization" is called homomorphic encryption. This technique allows the computation of cyphertexts, where encrypted data can be subject to computation and the generated result is the same as when it would have been performed on the unencrypted data.[98] In itself it will not lead to GDPR compliance but in addition with some of the other techniques described here, it might pull the application over the threshold of what is considered anonymization. Other possible solutions might come from state channels where information is only shared with outside parties in case of a dispute,[99] ring signatures that hide transactions by tying a transaction to multiple private keys or the addition of noise in the data by adding multiple transactions together (you have seen several examples of this technique throughout this book). It is clear that only by combining several of these techniques you can hope to achieve GDPR compliance, but again, this is to this day open to uncertainty.

An idea launched by some is the use of chameleon-hash functions with ephemeral trapdoors which would allow the creation of editable blockchains where data could later be adapted or modified.[100] Although this might lead to GDPR compliance, why would you still use a blockchain application in this case? Other techniques can be thought of to protect personal data in a blockchain environment but for now they all operate in a legally uncertain environment. It has also been mentioned in some comments that the techniques described above can also lead to undesirable outcomes when we

[96]Bacon J et al (2018), 'Blockchain Demystified: A Technical and Legal Introduction to Distributed and Centralised Ledgers' Richmond Journal of Law and Technology 1, 63

[97]Böhme R and Pesch P (2017), "Technische Grundlagen und datenschutzrechtliche Fragen der Blockchain Technologie" 41 *Datenschutz und Datensicherheit* 473, 481

[98]Brakerski Z and Gentry C and Vaikuntanathan V (11 August 2011), Fully Homomorphic Encryption without Bootstrapping, https://eprint.iacr.org/2011/277

[99]Buterin Vitalik (15 January 2016), Privacy on the Blockchain https://blog.ethereum.org/2016/01/15/privacy-on-theblockchain/

[100]https://eprint.iacr.org/2017/011.pdf

look at other regulations and policies in place (such as money laundering, terrorism financing and others).

Consent is yet another possible issue when we look at the processing of personal data in a blockchain application. The GDPR regulation does not stipulate any specific form or requirements but clearly states that pre-ticked boxes or silence cannot be seen as a form of consent.[101] Consent also has to cover all processing activities that are to be carried out, so that consent has to be given for each form of processing the party intends. You should also know that in an electronic context, the request for consent must be clear, concise and not unnecessarily disruptive to the use of the service for which it is provided and it can only be seen as "freely given" if the data subject has a genuine and free choice and is able to refuse or withdraw consent without detriment. The regulation also stipulates that the consent can only be seen as informed if the data subject knows the controller's identity.[102] You can clearly see that some of these requirements form no problem when we consider blockchain technology, while others can lead to even more and deeper issues (think about the identity of the controller or the withdrawal of consent and the consequences of this action). There can be a case where consent cannot be simply withdrawn, such as the lawful processing of personal data in a contractual or legal context. Personal data processing might be necessary to fulfill a contract, or the legal requirement to keep personal data a specific period of time. There can also be exceptions to protect the rights of other data subjects or public interests as a whole. Finally, there is the possibility of the "legitimate" interest of the data controller to process the data but this is very uncertain towards the future how this might be interpreted. Other principles that are considered in the regulation are fairness (processing should be lawful and fair), transparency (not meaning that the data controller should tell they are using blockchain technology but rather inform the data subject of the risks of the processing and the personal data that is being processed) and purpose limitation which means that the personal data should only be processed for the purpose it has been collected and nothing more. That final requirements means that the data processing should be specified sufficiently so that necessary data protection safeguards can be implemented, explicit as it must be sufficiently unambiguously expressed and legitimate as the processing should be in line with the broader legal principles of applicable law.[103] Further processing of personal data can be compliant even though it has not been originally communicated to the data subject, but this has to be analyzed on a case by case basis.

---

[101]Recital 32 GDPR
[102]Recital 42 GDPR
[103]4 Article 29 Working Party, Opinion 03/2013 on purpose limitation (WP 203) 00569/13/EN, 12-21

One final consideration must be taken for the use of smart contracts. You might think in themselves they don't prove an issue but you are mistaken. The data subject has the right not to be the subject to a decisions based solely on automated processing, including profiling, which produces legal effects concerning him or her or similarly significantly affects him or her.[104] The outcome from a smart contract can be seen as a decision, which makes it subject to the GDPR regulation. This prohibition does however not apply if it is necessary for the contract between the data subject and the data controller, is authorized by the Union or a member state law, or is based on the data subject's explicit consent.[105] As "explicit" consent is not clearly defined in the GDPR regulation and the other requirements are not always clear, also this is still open to further regulatory guidance.

So far we have only looked at blockchain technology and GDPR as 2 opposites, but this shouldn't always be the case. There is the idea of "data marketplaces" where both personal and non-personal data can be traded as a commodity.[106] The European Commission has stated that blockchain technology might be used to enable and power such a digital marketplace. This technology could indeed help in the management of data, the creation of contracts between bilateral parties and governance systems that might help to keep the entire process in check. The future might show that data sharing technologies can actually help the economy in the long run and prove successful (think about the Ocean protocol). Blockchain technology might also help to implement the "data protection by design" principles in the GDPR regulation.[107] Blockchain can help data subjects to monitor what is happening with their personal data and help them to decide who has access to their personal data. It could also help to monitor in line with the "purpose limitation principle" and help with the detection of data breaches or even fraud.

---

[104]Article 21 (1) GDPR

[105]Article 22 (2) GDPR

[106]7 European Commission (2017), 'Commission Staff Working Document on the free flow of data and emerging issues of the European Data Economy' SWD, 2 final 13

[107]European Parliament (27 November 2018) Report on Blockchain: a Forward-Looking Trade Policy (AB-0407/2018) para 14

Blockchain and Cryptocurrencies

By now you have seen and read quite a bit about blockchain technology. However, I want to close of this book with some final concepts that you should know and understand. These will allow you to zoom into some important aspects when you look at the crypto-markets and see how they function. Several new financial instruments have been devised with the creation of cryptocurrencies and existing financial assets have found their way into the world of cryptocurrencies.

A Short History of Crypto-Markets

The history of cryptocurrencies and assets is strongly linked to the history of the blockchain technology itself, or at least it was in the beginning. Sadly, the reputation of the technology was tarnished when the markets crashed after the huge hype created in 2018-2019.[1] As we saw in Chapter 1, everything starts in October 2008, when an unknown individual called Satoshi Nakamoto released their whitepaper describing Bitcoin. The initial idea sparked both interest and skepticism and the first blockchain block ever, the Bitcoin genesis block, was released in January 2009. It was also in this month that the first transaction took place, between Satoshi Nakamoto and a developer named

---

[1] https://docs.google.com/document/d/1cxEwTbfIWBg8n6uQYK4m3ITsKsebrqVYQ-Ps1fEcXB0/edit#heading=h.yt4ufl41p1v4

© Stijn Van Hijfte 2020
S. Van Hijfte, *Decoding Blockchain for Business*,
https://doi.org/10.1007/978-1-4842-6137-8_5

Hal Finney. This was the beginning of the cryptocurrency world. In October 2009, there was a first valuation of Bitcoin with the New Liberty Standard, where $1 = 1,309 BTC. The first Bitcoin market, *dwdollar*, was established in February 2010. For the first time ever, other participants could buy and sell the cryptocurrency.

In May 2010, a notable milestones takes place in the Bitcoin world, still known to many enthusiasts and participants of the cryptocurrency world. Laslo Hanyecz spends about 10,000 BTC to buy a pizza from Papa John's. It was the first real-world transaction where the cryptocurrency was used to buy something material. This height in perception would be crushed a couple of months later (August 2010) when first there was a hack that maliciously acted on a vulnerability in the Bitcoin network, leading to the generation of 182 billion Bitcoins. The value of the cryptocurrency is reduced to almost nothing. The perception of Bitcoin would undergo even more damage when there were more vulnerabilities discovered in September of that year, while in October there was a report suggesting that Bitcoin could be used for money laundering and financing terrorist activities.[2] Still, in November of 2010, the market would reach a value of $1 million USD (at a valuation of $0.50/BTC).

In 2011, the first price surge of Bitcoin takes place, which leads to a valuation in June of $31/BTC (starting from parity in January). Fast forward to June 2013, when the market reaches a capitalization of $ 1billion. It is also around this time that the first regulation is released by the U.S. Financial Crimes Enforcement Network. A couple of months later, another major theft took place,[3] followed by another security breach, crushing the value of Bitcoin to $0.01. In August of the same year, U.S. federal judge Mazzant[4] first states that Bitcoin can be used as a currency to be exchanged for goods and services. At the same time, Bloomberg starts with the integration of Bitcoin data in its portal, increasing the acceptance of the cryptocurrency.[5]

The first major divide occurs in November-December, 2013. While the U.S. Senate starts their first hearings on Bitcoin, the Federal Reserve chairman, Ben Bernanke, gives his blessing and support for the network. In China, on the other hand, the first ban is imposed on financial institutions from handling Bitcoin transactions.[6] In 2014, overstock.com becomes the first large retailer to accept Bitcoin payments, while Elliptic launched the first insured Bitcoin storage service. Later that year, the Silk Road is closed and its Bitcoins (29,000)

---

[2]Silkroad started to accept Bitcoins as a method of payment a couple of months later. It is now clear for everyone that this was a drug trafficking network (among other things).
[3]Allinvain had 25,000 BTC stolen from his wallet.
[4]www.forbes.com/sites/kashmirhill/2013/08/07/federal-judge-rules-bitcoin-is-real-money/
[5]www.cityam.com/bloomberg-confirms-it-internally-testing-bitcoin-ticker/
[6]www.bloomberg.com/news/articles/2013-12-05/china-s-pboc-bans-financial-companies-from-bitcoin-transactions

are being sold by the U.S. government.[7] In New Jersey the first regulated Bitcoin investment fund (GABI) received its certification.[8] By the end of the year, TeraExchange starts with the first Bitcoin-derived transactions on a regulated exchange. This meant further integration of the currency in the standard ways of working and acceptance by the main financial institutions.

In 2015, the New York Stock Exchange becomes one of the investors behind Coinbase, the UK Treasury starts a call for information on digital currency, and Barclays starts to accept Bitcoin as well. The next year, the cabinet of Japan recognizes virtual currencies as having a similar function as regular currencies and Bidorbuy in South Africa starts to accept Bitcoin as payments together with Steam. In August, a new major hack takes place with Bitfinex. Later in 2016, the Swiss railway operator SBB would accept Bitcoin in their ticket machines.

The year 2017 saw an even further surge in stores accepting Bitcoin and other cryptocurrencies, whereby Russia and Norway accept, legalize, and further integrate Bitcoin payment accounts. In both 2018 and 2019, more and more stores started accepting cryptocurrencies, but they are still in the corner when compared to regular currencies. These years have also seen further crashes and rises in the market. With the appearance of the Coronavirus, both the regular market and the cryptocurrency market have seen serious decline. Only time will tell how it will affect these markets in the long run.

Cryptocurrency Markets

The cryptocurrency market is a volatile market that has been characterized in the last years with steep rises and falls. Contrary to other financial markets, cryptocurrency markets are characterized by their decentralized nature. This means that they depend on peer-to-peer markets, where transactions are propagated through nodes and eventually stored in blocks. This also means that there is no central authority or government that is backing the currency.

Similar to other markets, the laws of supply and demand influence the price of cryptocurrencies. The total number of coins and the rate at which they are released or destroyed are the dominant factors dominating supply. You have cryptocurrencies such as Bitcoin, which have a limited total supply (only 21 million Bitcoins be mined, after this point it becomes impossible because of the limitations implemented in the algorithm of the network). This is completely different from Ethereum, which doesn't cap the total number of Ether that can be mined. Ripple is a third example where more of the cryptocurrency is released in several rounds.

---

[7]www.theguardian.com/technology/2014/jun/24/us-auction-seized-silk-road-bitcoins

[8]www.bbc.com/news/world-europe-jersey-28247796

Market capitalization (supply and demand) is a second factor that determines the value of the cryptocurrency. The more investors are interested in a certain cryptocurrency, the more demand will increase and hence the value of the cryptocurrency will rise. Other factors include the integration of cryptocurrencies as a usable means of payment in (online) stores and e-commerce payment systems. The greater the general acceptance of a specific cryptocurrency, the more likely the value of the currency itself will increase.

Changes in regulation—such as acceptance of cryptocurrencies as a legitimate means of payment or investment, creating a framework for ICOs, and further enabling investments in blockchain infrastructure—greatly influence the value of cryptocurrencies (as we saw with the crash in 2018). Others factors are press coverage, investor acceptance, and the growth of interesting blockchain use cases. Finally, prosecution of those who lure investors into nonexistent cryptocurrencies, creating fake ICOs and stealing investor funds, further increases the value of legitimate cryptocurrencies.

A second aspect of the crypto-world is the existence of crypto-assets. Cryptocurrencies are one aspect of crypto-assets, but you also have other digital assets that can be traded. Next to cryptocurrencies, you have platform tokens, or crypto-commodities, utility tokens, and transactional tokens. Ether (from the Ethereum network) is considered a platform token, as the platform can be used to create decentralized applications. Utility tokens exist on top of other platforms such as Ethereum. These tokens have been developed with a specific use case in mind. Finally, there are transactional tokens. Examples are Ripple, IOTA, and Stellar. These tokens are used to enable cross-border payments.

Next to cryptocurrencies, derivatives trading has also been created. These financial instruments play into the value of cryptocurrencies and how they change over time. There are options and other instruments out there that are even more high risk but promise high return. If these instruments are used and traded in high amounts, they can introduce even more uncertainty in already volatile markets.

You should understand that people will keep on finding new ways to create financial instruments. Understanding these instruments and the markets they function in is crucial for any investor.

Some Core Cryptocurrency Concepts

In this section, we cover core concepts that you will almost certainly hear or read about if you decide to enter the cryptocurrency market. Understanding these core concepts will help you not only better understand these markets but also understand the possible issues with these markets.

Atomic Transactions

Atomic swaps are cryptocurrency transactions that happen peer-to-peer without needing a third party such as an exchange. The first atomic swap took place on September 20, 2017 between Decred and Litecoin.[9] These transactions can take place in several ways—either directly between the separate blockchains even though they have different native coins, or by using off-chain channels. These transactions between different cryptocurrencies make the entire cryptocurrency system even more flexible.

With the advent of atomic swaps, we enter the possibility of a world with fee-less exchanges. These (on-chain) swaps can take place because the participants work based on a shared secret. Similar to the Lightning network (which is a network on top of the Bitcoin network to improve scalability and transaction speed), here we similarly use hashed time-locked contracts (HTLCs). In short, when we have two participants that want to exchange two different types of cryptocurrencies, they open a payment channel. The first participant creates a payment address. There is a deposit on this address by the first participant and, after this, a value is created. This value is the key, while the hash of the value is the lock. The first participant sends the hash to the second participant. The second participant generates an address but uses the hash they received to do this. They then send their coins to the second address.

Still following? Well, only the first participant can unlock the second address by using their value. This can be done by signing the transaction for the second participant's address. Similarly, the second participant signs a transaction for the first participant's address. One problem: the second participant doesn't have the value to unlock their new coins. This value is revealed when the first participant signs their transaction. This way, the second participant can unlock the account.

The assumptions here are that both currencies support hashed time-locked contracts. Furthermore, they need to have the same hashing algorithm. When this is not the case, atomic swaps between the currencies simply cannot happen. Of course, one could try to achieve swaps by using several steps (direct swap between BTC and ETH isn't possible but using DOGE is). Off-chain transactions take place via a layer 2 protocol such as the Lightning network.

In practice, the Komodo platform and blockchain.io are both focusing on atomic swaps between several parties.

---

[9]https://blockgeeks.com/guides/atomic-swaps/

The ICO

The ICO (initial coin offering) is the crowd sale of new cryptocurrencies to possible investors.[10] In the past years, there was almost regulation making it an attractive way to lure investors. However, this has also allowed a number of conmen to enter the scene, certainly during the high days of the crypto-bubble. Investors were no longer thoroughly checking about what they were investing, and just wanted to profit as well from the major profits that were being made in the crypto-market. Some of the ICOs were purely based on ideas, without anything else, and were able to reap in millions without anything concrete to match. Some of these projects became a success, but most ICOs that had nothing than an idea behind them led to nothing. To give you an idea, in about 4.5 months in 2018, 6.3 billion USD were raised with ICOs! Table 5-1 shows some of the biggest ICO scams (to date).[11]

Table 5-1. Biggest ICO Scams to Date

Scam Name	Amount of Money Scammed (USD)
Pincoin and iFan	660,000,000
CentraTech	32,000,000
Onecoin	30,000,000
Plexcoin	15,000,000
Bitcard	5,000,000
Opair and Ebitz	2,900,000
Benebit	2,700,000
Bitconnect	700,000
Confido	375,000
REcoin and DRC	300,000
Ponzicoin	250,000
Karbon	200,000

Does this mean that every ICO is a scam? Of course not, but just as with regular investments, it is up to you to perform due diligence, concerning the projects and the companies behind an ICO, but also concerning the regulation and the possible pitfalls. This relates to personal liability as well (remember the DAO case!). Research the development team behind an ICO project as well. It is not an uncommon tactic to invent fake founders and biographies to give a project more legitimacy. Even if the development team is real, is their

---

[10]https://blockgeeks.com/guides/initial-coin-offering/
[11]https://medium.com/@tozex/the-five-biggest-ico-scams-54967ec92b87

experience real?[12] Next, read the whitepaper thoroughly. Is the documentation reasonable? Can they achieve what they want to achieve? Do you see this project going somewhere? And even if there is a convincing whitepaper (as was the case with Plexcoin), do not immediately trust them. Another red flag is if you cannot clearly follow the ICO process. For a legitimate company, it shouldn't be too hard to show how the process works and show the progress during the sale. If they hide this or make it extremely difficult to understand, you should know something is wrong. But finally, and I cannot state this clear enough, always exercise caution when considering investing in an ICO. Getting rich quick is always a nice idea, but the likelihood of it happening is really small. If something sounds too good to be true, it probably is.

While the first ICO ever was probably the sale of Ripple in early 2013, it was the Ethereum ICO in 2014 that was able to draw the public's attention, because it raised 18.4 million USD. What did the investors receive in return? More often than not, the answer is "tokens," which can refer to value, stake, voting rights, or anything else for that matter. When you ask the SEC (Securities and Exchange Commission), there are only two types: security tokens and utility tokens.

Security tokens are identified using the Howey test, which consists of three questions:

- Is it an investment of money?
- Is the investment in a common enterprise?
- Is there an expectation of profit from the work of the promoters of the third party?

If not all these questions can be answered positively, you are dealing with a utility token. These tokens give holders the right to use the network or take advantage of the network by voting.

So why do projects start an ICO in the first place? Most importantly because they wouldn't be able to start an IPO (initial public offering). The ICO allows them to have a shot at their project, without having to go through all the regulatory requirements linked to an IPO. But probably the most important advantage is the strong link that is created between a project and the community. As most of these projects also need that same community to exist and flourish, ICOs deliver the perfect platform to create a mutual, beneficial relationship. Table 5-2 shows the ICOs with the highest returns to date.

---

[12]www.investopedia.com/tech/how-identify-cryptocurrency-and-ico-scams/

Table 5-2. ICOs with the Highest Returns to Date

Name	ROI
NXT	1,265,555%
Iota	424,084%
NEO	378,453%
Ethereum	279,843%
Spectrecoin	149,806%
Stratis	102,338%
Ark	37,805%
Lisk	26,367%
DixigDAO	12,044%
QTUM	9,225%

However, you should also consider the disadvantages, and there are quite a few. As mentioned, there are scammers out there who are waiting to take advantage of people not looking into the details. On top of that, even if the development team behind a project is genuine, 90% of startups still fail! Another disadvantage is the appearance of "crypto-whales," which are investors that immediately buy huge bulks of the ICO, cutting in line by paying high amounts of transaction fees, thereby destroying the idea of decentralization. An example is the BAT ICO, where 35 million USD was raised in 24 seconds by a few investors.

A fourth disadvantage is the popularity of certain ICOs that effectively clog up the network, thereby preventing investors from participating or even completely cutting out the ICO! Finally, I should also mention the security of ICOs and security platforms as a whole. In the past, several infamous hacks have taken place, leading to the theft of millions. Due to the nature of cryptocurrencies, there will always be security measures that you have to take into consideration and certainly with something that is new or untested, you can imagine that there are flaws that have been overlooked by even the best developers.

Even though ICOs still take place, you should also know that regulatory bodies are taking a deeper interest in them. The SEC forces new ICOs to declare if they are a security and China and India have banned ICOs all together. Within the EU, the ICOs have to meet the AML/KYC regulations that are in place. It is seen as a high-risk investment that should be strongly regulated to protect the investors. However, the EU believes that it should support innovation and has therefore not banned the practice.[13] The future will show how regulation changes over time and how ICOs might evolve.

Fractional Reserve Banking and Bitcoin

There have been some discussions on the concept of fractional reserve banking and the use of Bitcoin (or any other cryptocurrency for that matter). Basically, you have two major views looking at the concept: the Keynesian and the Austrian view.[14] From the first perspective, there is no real difference from any other currency. Banks can still present customers any token as "available for withdrawal," while at the same time making them available for loans for different customers.

Of course, the bank is responsible for keeping a sufficient supply in deposit to make sure it can handle the withdrawals and payments from the customers. These banks would need to rely on their own reserves, as a central bank would not be able to help them in case of a default. If we take Bitcoin as an example, we can understand that, even though there is a maximum supply of 21 million Bitcoin, with the use of fractional banking, the Bitcoin money supply can be multiplied by the money multiplier. Some supporters of the idea of fractional reserve banking with Bitcoin (or any cryptocurrency for that matter) state that this limited supply could make it better for fractional reserve banking than any other currency, as those are traditionally more likely to become inflationary, where a currency with a limited supply is more likely to be deflationary.

The Austrian viewpoint takes a different approach. For fractional banking to have an effect on the money supply, the debt instruments used by the bank must be accepted if they were themselves proper money. In the past, there were some other forms of Bitcoin, such as Casascius physical Bitcoins (stopped in 2013) and Bitbills (stopped in 2012). In the past, there have been some other debt instrument issuances, but these often led to issues as they were restricted to a narrow field of uses. The transactions happening outside of the Bitcoin network are not compatible with it. In the past there have also been issues with eliminating the excess instruments (Mt. Gox hack in June 2011), bankruptcy (mybitcoin), or investor bailout. Based on the previous information, we have to consider over-issuance, the general acceptance of debt instruments, and the market price of the debt instruments at a different rate than the reserve ratio of the issuer.

So, is it possible to create a fractional reserve banking system with a cryptocurrency? Several views have been issued in the past, stating that this can only be an illusion if you look at the background of cryptocurrencies, the

---

[13]www.cyberius.com/blog/news/european-regulations-on-icos/
[14]https://en.bitcoin.it/wiki/Fractional_Reserve_Banking_and_Bitcoin

regulatory issues, combined with issues related to scalability and transparency. Others do believe in the system, such as the reports that MasterCard has been trying to patent cryptocurrency fractional reserve banking.[15] One of the key ingredients for such a system to emerge and to become successful is that a cryptocurrency (or more than one) should emerge as a widely accepted means of payment. The same cryptocurrency would have to be used for high-value transactions between large institutions, which are two though requirements for a cryptocurrency today.

Other impacts of fractional reserve banking on cryptocurrencies is the influence on price. By using fractional reserve banking, you are likely to reduce the value of the cryptocurrency for investors that are holding on to a certain deposit. This means that it might be against their interests to support these practices. There are several ways to offset these developments. One is that the maximum amount of cryptocurrency deposits through fractional reserve banking must be a finite multiple of the amount of outstanding cryptocurrency. Another is that investors might decide to hold more of the fractional reserve banking cryptocurrency deposits than they would of the underlying cryptocurrency.

As you can see, there are several ways to discuss the theoretical possibility of fractional reserve banking with a cryptocurrency, but these remain theoretical for the time being. The underlying factors that need to be fulfilled before one might even consider fractional reserve banking are quite onerous. Even as a best case, it would be risky. Combine this with regulatory issues, the problem of clear oversight by any type of government, and the absence of clear insurance for investors, and it becomes pretty clear that this doesn't seem realistic in the near future. Central banks and governments are better suited to deal with the risks introduced by "classic" currencies and banks, while cryptocurrencies bring a whole set of risks of their own.

Stablecoins

Stablecoins are another important aspect of the blockchain world and cryptocurrencies that we should take into account. These are specifically designed to reduce the volatility of cryptocurrencies and are commonly pegged to a stable asset or basket of assets.[16] These currencies can be backed by commodities, fiat, or other cryptocurrencies.

A first example is the Digix Gold Token, which is backed by gold. Introducing a gold standard to the cryptocurrency world, these tokens are clearly linked and backed by a precious metal, which provides more security than stablecoins backed by either fiat or other cryptocurrencies.[17]

---

[15]www.frbatlanta.org/cenfis/publications/notesfromthevault/04-fractional-reserve-cryptocurrency-banks-2019-04-25
[16]https://en.wikipedia.org/wiki/Stablecoin
[17]https://digix.global/

Fiat-backed stablecoins base their value on a pegged fiat currency, where a third-party (regulated financial entity) holds the value of the backing fiat. These tokens can be traded and redeemed for the backing currency at the issuer. One should not underestimate the cost of such a peg, as you should take into consideration the cost of maintaining the backing reserve, legal compliance, maintaining licenses, audits, and more. TrustToken is a company that specializes in stablecoins, such as TrueUSD, TrueGBP, TrueAUD, and more.[18] It uses multiple third-party financial institutions to maintain its peg to these currencies and claims to have passed several security audits in the past.[19]

A second and much more controversial fiat-backed stablecoin is called Tether. The whitepaper was published in January 2012 by J.R. Willett, and it describes a new cryptocurrency on top of the Bitcoin network. By using Mastercoin and the Mastercoin foundation (now the Omni foundation), he created (together with Brock Pierce) the Tether cryptocurrency. It used to claim that it was backed by USD, but changed its statement on March 14, 2019.[20] Since that date, it also includes loans to affiliate companies, therefore immediately jeopardizing its status as a stablecoin.

Even worse, the New York attorney general alleges that Bitfinex used Tether reserves up to 850 million USD to cover up their own missing funds, which occurred in mid-2018 and hadn't been disclosed publicly.[21] Tether Limited now even claims that Tether owners have no contractual rights or legal claims that the Tethers will be exchanged for USD. On April 30, 2019, Tether Limited's lawyer claimed that each Tether was backed by $0.74 in cash and cash equivalents.[22]

The company has also been accused of not providing the promised audit results of their adequate results backing Tether, manipulation of the Bitcoin price, the unclear relationship with the Bitfinex exchange (the Paradise papers leak suggests a link, as Philip Potter and Giancarlo Devasini were responsible for setting up Tether Holdings Limited in the British Virgin Islands in 2014; next to these leads, there is also the fact that the spokesperson for Bitfinex and Tether has stated that the CEO of both is Jan Ludovicus van der Velde[23]), and the lack of a long-term banking relationship (there were transactions

---

[18]www.trusttoken.com/currencies

[19]www.coindesk.com/trusttoken-says-it-passed-3-security-audits-with-no-bugs-found

[20]www.forbes.com/sites/francescoppola/2019/03/14/tethers-u-s-dollar-peg-is-no-longer-credible/#3b108717451b

[21]www.wsj.com/articles/bitfinex-used-tether-reserves-to-mask-missing-850-million-probe-finds-11556227031

[22]www.bloomberg.com/news/articles/2019-04-30/tether-says-stablecoin-is-only-backed-74-by-cash-securities

[23]www.bloomberg.com/news/articles/2018-01-30/crypto-exchange-bitfinex-tether-said-to-get-subpoenaed-by-cftc

through a Taiwanese bank, back through Wells Fargo).[24] In 2017, other Tether coins were issued—Euro Tether on Bitcoin's omni layer, and USD and Euro Tether as ERC-20 tokens on the Ethereum network.

The case of Tether has clearly shown that stablecoins cannot be trusted blindly. However, you should understand the popularity of Tether, as it is the most traded cryptocurrency when we talk about daily trading volumes. It is very popular in Asia and is even feared to clog up the Ethereum network because of the number of transactions that are taking place every day.

Another player that wants to fill the gap and create a major stablecoin is Facebook, with its "Libra" project. The launch of Libra (formerly known as GlobalCoin or Facebook coin) is projected in 2020 at the earliest, so it doesn't exist yet, but there has been already some controversy surrounding the project. The project started in 2017 with Morgan Beller working on Facebook's blockchain initiative (later on David Marcus and Kevin Well joined the project).[25] By February 2019, there were already about 50 engineers working on the project in a completely separate division.

The project was met with a lot of criticism, also relating to the questionable reputation Facebook has when it comes to privacy of its users. There were some scandals in the past showing that the company takes privacy regulation quite lightly (Cambridge Analytica comes to mind), so a cryptocurrency linked to this Internet giant seems to be the next step in controlling our personal data. Other concerns are linked to the sheer size of the company and the number of users, making it rival many fiat currencies, but without the checks and balances that are in place for centralized currencies. Libra also wouldn't be a decentralized currency but would use a centralized system, with the "Libra association" in Geneva, Switzerland at its core. The bucket behind Libra would consist 50% USD, 18% Euro, 14% Japanese yen, 11% Pound sterling, and 7% Singapore dollar.

The launch of the currency has been stopped due to the criticism received from the public and many regulatory institutions. On September 4, Mark Zuckerberg announced that the launch would be postponed until all (United States) regulatory concerns have been dealt with.[26] Originally, the plans were supported by a number of big and important payment parties. PayPal left the project on October 4, 2019, while eBay, MasterCard, Stripe,

---

[24]www.wsj.com/articles/the-mystery-behind-tether-the-crypto-worlds-digital-dollar-1534089601

[25]www.cnbc.com/2019/07/20/facebook-libra-partly-created-by-female-engineer-morgan-beller.html

[26]www.washingtonpost.com/technology/2019/09/19/facebooks-mark-zuckerberg-dined-with-lawmakers-last-night-privacy-cryptocurrency-were-menu/

Visa, and Mercado Pago left on October 11, with Bookings Holdings following on the 14th. A number of companies still support the association, such as Uber, Spotify, Lyft, PayU, Coinbase, and many others.

The response in the United States was quite harsh, with President Trump claiming that Facebook would have to adhere to Banking regulation and questioning if they would want to proceed with the project.[27] The response in Europe, and most notably in France, was even more harsh, with the French finance minister Bruno Le Maire claiming that Libra could be a threat to monetary sovereignty of nations and should therefore not be allowed to be developed. He also went on to state that it might incorporate abuse of marketing dominance and could introduce systemic financial risks. German MEP Markus Feber also warned that Facebook could become a shadow bank with the power it would have over Libra.

The government of Japan has also started an investigation in how Libra might affect the monetary policy and financial regulation. Finally, there were the alarming sounds from Switzerland, where the Federal Data Protection and Information Commissioner stated that it had never heard from Facebook at all (this while David Markus claimed before the U.S. Senate that they would oversee the project).

Finally, there are also cryptocurrency-backed stablecoins. While these are very similar to fiat-backed cryptocurrencies, the main difference lies in the fact that crypto-backed stablecoins use smart contracts in a decentralized fashion to back their coins.[28] These also often allow users to take out loans against a smart contract, locking in a certain amount of collateral. These smart contracts may liquidate the user's loan if the collateral decreases too close to the value of their withdrawal. You can immediately sense that these coins require more implementation effort via coding, introducing the risk of bugs and possible exploits. You used to have the DAI Maker stablecoin (which has currently been transformed into a fiat-backed stablecoin, pegged to USD), but the Synthetix company still offers, next to fiat-backed stablecoins, cryptocurrency-backed stablecoins.

One final example we should look into are the seigniorage-style stablecoins, which are not backed by any asset. Here, there are algorithms in place that regulate the money supply so that they can ensure that the currency maintains a certain price. One project that wanted to achieve this is called "Basis," but it was eventually shut down because of the U.S. securities regulations that would have applied to the project.[29]

---

[27]https://libra.org/en-US/
[28]https://masterthecrypto.com/guide-to-stablecoin-types-of-stablecoins/
[29]www.basis.io/

Digital Twins and Blockchain

Something that has also gotten some extra attention in recent years is the creation of digital twins to protect brands against counterfeiting.[30] Digital twins are of course not only limited to blockchain technology, as we all know with our digital identities. However, blockchain platforms offer a new way of storing a digital twin in a secure manner and without a centralized point of control or single point of failure.

Blockchain offers the possibility to add data and follow the process of an asset, without the possibility to simply modify or corrupt the data that has been stored. Combine this idea with that of digital certificates or blockchain-linked identities and you are able to design a process to follow up on assets, services, and products all over the world. The concept of non-fungible tokens takes a prominent role here, as these represent the asset in the digital world.

Now, where can these digital twins prove their worth? A very interesting example is that of pharmaceuticals and counterfeited products. By creating digital twins on the blockchain, one can easily follow a product from producer to consumer, and any product not matching the data in the system can be tagged as at least suspicious. This could add an extra layer to the current battle against drug abuse and medicine counterfeiting. A second example is that of notary services for the real estate market, where one could buy or sell a house based on the digital twin that is available on the blockchain.

Based on the previous examples, it should be fairly simple for you to think about some other examples where digital twins could prove to be useful or interesting and could enhance the current way of working. As with any decentralized technology, a lot will depend on the cooperation of different parties within the process, to make these digital trends a success.

Luxtag is an example of a company focusing on product and asset security.[31] They offer a base API to follow your product as a digital twin, but also tamper-proof credentials.

Blockchain and Digital Identity

A common issue in our world today is that of personal identity. Even though it has been identified as a basic human right in the UN's convention on the rights of the child, we often find problems in many countries. These relate to places that have been faced with war, poverty, or lack of governance. Without some basic personal information, you are limited in almost every

---

[30]https://medium.com/luxtag-live-tokenized-assets-on-blockchain/how-creating-digital-twins-on-blockchain-will-protect-brands-3ada31b5fb2f
[31]www.luxtag.io/

way, as you cannot own property, vote, receive government services, have a bank account, find employment, ask for protection, or pursue anything else for that matter.[32]

As it currently works, centralized institutions need to give you an identity, and if they do so, they can still mishandle your data. A final consideration is the possibility of identity theft, which is always looming in the modern world. If you look at the case of refugees, it is often difficult to verify their identity, their back story, and their credentials, certainly when they come from a nation at war with the destruction of information and the impossibility of verification. According to the World Bank Group's 2018 #ID4D Global Dataset, almost 1 billion people around the globe struggle proving who they are![33] On top of that, about 1.7 billion people don't have a bank account.[34] Blockchain solutions might not only provide a means of payment to people who have been left out of the centralized solutions of the modern world, but they might also help them to finally prove their identities.

How could it facilitate the current challenges of digital identity? Well, when we think about identity theft, it comes down to how we make it very difficult to use the same identity twice for two different people. Trying to use the same digital unit twice is also known as the "double spending" issue. Similarly to preventing double spending, the blockchain technology could prevent the double use of a single identity by rogue elements in the system. By using hashes, one could also make sure that digital files haven't been tampered with, otherwise one will immediately see that something has been changed in the data, thereby proving that they are no longer dealing with the original document. Finally, there is the malicious intent one could have in the system when trying to perform certain processes. By using decentralized consensus, these processes can be stopped in the system, protecting participants from these attackers.

Most importantly, if we could agree on one decentralized system spanning the world, identity would no longer pose a problem. We would have irreversible proof of each person, without having to question whether the data is correct or whether the data belongs to a different person. Of course, this is something that will not be happening tomorrow, but several implementations are working on digital identity with blockchain technology, such as the Sovrin foundation (also behind Hyperledger Indy), Civic, and uPort.

---

[32]https://blockgeeks.com/guides/blockchain-and-digital-identity-ultimate-guide/
[33]https://blogs.worldbank.org/voices/global-identification-challenge-who-are-1-billion-people-without-proof-identity
[34]https://globalfindex.worldbank.org/

Where Do Cryptocurrencies Get Their Value?

An important question asked by people new to the cryptocurrency space is where cryptocurrencies derive their value. This very much depends on the type and kind of token you are dealing with. As we mentioned, there are the stablecoins, which try to peg to a certain asset, fiat currency, or cryptocurrency (or a bucket of those). These derive their value from the peg they are trying to maintain, but we have seen that this is not always successful, which immediately leads to the devaluation of the token.

A lot of people will say that it simply comes down to supply and demand. And to a certain extent, this is certainly true. As we have seen in the past (and still today), fluctuations in price can be clearly linked to the demand for certain tokens, just as the vanishing demand for a specific cryptocurrency might destroy its price. However, there are some other aspects that we should take into consideration when we look at possible drivers of the value of a specific token.

When we move away from stablecoins to more general cryptocurrencies, there are a couple of factors that we have to consider. First of all, these tokens can be seen both as a medium of exchange and as a store of value.[35] When we extrapolate from the Bitcoin case, the store of value valuation of a certain cryptocurrency is linked to its power as a medium of exchange. If a token does not achieve success as a medium of exchange, it will not be able to act as a store of value. A second consideration is the legitimacy of cryptocurrencies that might increase/decrease over time, leading to more or less adoption of these tokens, which in turn has an impact on their volatility. Thirdly, we have to look into the appearance of speculative valuation bubbles. These reduce the attractiveness of these currencies for participants interested in stable environments. Other possible considerations are whether some of these coins might be used for fractional reserve banking (or not), and if there is a limited or limitless supply of these tokens. You could also take into consideration the energy spent to mine a token and the value created in other processes (i.e., contributions to science or specific industries). Finally, some tokens represent a certain service or product, such as Internet access, media distribution, voting rights, and more.

Only when you take all these drivers into account, together with a healthy (and hopefully growing) interest from a supporting community, can you try to understand how the value of certain cryptocurrencies is derived, and how their value might change in the future.

---

[35]www.investopedia.com/ask/answers/100314/why-do-bitcoins-have-value.asp

Crypto Dust

Crypto dust is something specific to the cryptocurrency world, but something you should certainly be aware of. As you might have guessed, *dust* refers to tiny pieces of value of a certain token. These tiny outputs are generated after a number of transactions and eventually require more fees to be transacted than their actual value. This is because these tiny transactions take up just as much space on the blockchain as large transactions, leading to the discrepancy between the fee that needs to be paid and the actual value of the transaction.[36]

As you can imagine, for many cryptocurrencies, the transaction fee is linked to the popularity and congestion of the network. This means that a certain value today might not pose a problem, while tomorrow it might become crypto dust. The only way to fix the issue with dust is by collecting enough of these dust values and consolidating them into one transaction by lumping them together. This technique depends on the wallet you are using and the cryptocurrency that you want to consolidate. The only possible issue with this is the price you pay: your privacy. As you are sending a lot of dust from different change addresses to your main wallet account, it can become apparent to other participants that these are linked to you as well. Certainly if you have been through a KYC (Know Your Customer) process that verifies your identity (necessary for financial institutions to fight financial crime), the link can easily be made.

Linked to this issue are so-called "dusting attacks," which are used to determine participants' identities.[37] This attack consists of dust transactions that are sent to the victims' wallets. They keep these transactions in a log and after a while the attackers can link several wallets together and determine the identity of the person behind a certain wallet. Certain wallets, such as the Samourai wallet, now flag dust transactions as suspicious by default to protect their users.

Exchanges and Attacks

When we talk about cryptocurrency exchanges, we talk about online platforms that allow participants to exchange a digital asset for another based on the market value of these assets.[38] You should not confuse these exchanges with wallets or wallet brokerages, which allow you to buy or sell a small range of cryptocurrencies, which in turn can be exchanged for other tokens. Most exchanges will allow you to trade one token for another, while some others will still allow you to trade for a limited number of fiat currencies (an example is Kraken).

---

[36]www.coindesk.com/bitcoin-dust-tell-get-rid
[37]www.binance.vision/nl/security/what-is-a-dusting-attack
[38]www.ethos.io/what-are-cryptocurrency-exchanges/

When you want to start using these exchanges as well, or start trading cryptocurrencies, you should start by setting up your own online account. One example where you can do this is Coinbase. Of course you can use any other online service but you should always consider the safety of these online services, so do your research before you open an account. You want to make sure that your invested funds don't just suddenly disappear. There are also lists available online, such as in Belgium where the FSMA has published a non-exhaustive list of websites linked to fraud.

Nevertheless, once you have set up your account, you will most probably only be able to buy specific cryptocurrencies (i.e. Bitcoin and Ether). If you want to buy something else, you will have to open an account on an exchange. There, you can trade the Ether or Bitcoin you bought for other tokens. With most of these other tokens, it is not possible to simply convert them back to fiat if you want to cash out (or at least not for now). This means you have to convert them back to Ether or Bitcoin first, which then can be exchanged for fiat currency. On top of that, you will have to take into account local regulations when it comes to profit from trading and cryptocurrencies in general.

All of this seems fairly easy to understand. So why are these exchanges so often victims of cyberattacks?[39] Well, first of all, these exchanges have to hold large amounts of cryptocurrencies to ensure their liquidity (immediately proving that criminals are lured by the money they might make if they are successful). There are also a lot of transactions happening. The investments in cybersecurity are often limited, as these companies need their cash to grow and innovate, and cashing out stolen cryptocurrencies is often a whole lot easier than doing so with fiat currency. This makes it even more attractive to prospective criminals.

A lot of people seem to have the idea that to attack such an exchange, very specific attack vectors need to be used to be successful. In reality we are dealing with a web service that is susceptible to a lot of the same attacks as any other web service, meaning that there is a range of server-side and client-side attacks that can be executed. When we look at the report provided by hackernoon, we can see that there are four sections of attacks that are relevant for exchanges (when they look at those exchanges that have a daily trade value of at least $100,000): user security, domain and registrar security, web security, and DoS protection.[40]

I will not go into detail about all the possible attack vectors for each of these sections, but it's important to understand that none of them got an A+ score, meaning that none of them are ideal. Only 21 got an A score while most got

---

[39]https://medium.com/block-to-basics/crypto-exchanges-why-are-they-being-hacked-so-often-b4346f281deb
[40]https://hackernoon.com/security-problems-of-crypto-exchanges-d5e2f595fb79

a B score, meaning that they have some issues. Table 5-3 shows the 21 exchanges that received an A score from the Hackernoon report.

Table 5-3. Exchanges with an A Score. Source: Hackernoon.com

Kraken	Cobinhood	Poloniex	BitMEX	Bitfinex	Bitlish	BitMart
BtcTurk	Coinbase Pro	GOPAX	Livecoin	UEX	HitBTC	BTC-Alpha
LiteBit	Exrates	Luno	Kucoin	Paribu	Bitso	Coinbe

To deal with these risks, several wallet solutions have been developed. A final example is the ZERO, developed by NGRAVE. While private keys stored by exchange platforms can be stolen during an attack, this wallet is locked away from any type of networking, has its own approach to key generation, and takes into account the use of QR codes. It is so far the only wallet that was able to obtain the EAL7 Common Criteria Certification.[41]

Cryptocurrency Market Capitalization

When you look into cryptocurrencies or start researching specific currencies, you will almost immediately come across charts discussing the market capitalization of a token.[42] What do they mean? Consider the example shown in Figure 5-1 to get a better understanding of this concept.

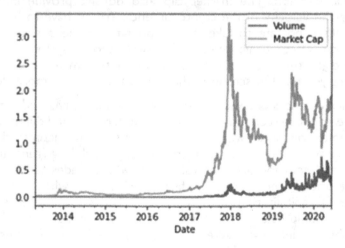

Figure 5-1. Cryptocurrency graph. Data Source: coinmarketcap.com

[41]https://medium.com/ngrave/ngraves-zero-hardware-wallet-is-the-coldest-wallet-of-them-all-483aa3d32a14
[42]https://coincentral.com/cryptocurrency-market-capitalization/

To get a better understanding of the price of a certain cryptocurrency, you should look at these charts. These charts can give you an idea of the market value, the volume, and the evolution over time of a currency, and you can also follow the impact of certain events. Analysts commonly use these charts to make informed investment decisions, as these charts show them the total current coins * current price.

These charts generally serve as an indicator of the amount of risk involved for investors. However, one should always take into account the fact that we are dealing with cryptocurrency markets, which inherently pose an increased risk for investors compared to other "classic" forms of investment. This might change in the future, and I am well aware that there will be people who do not agree with this view, but you should always take this into consideration when you plan to invest in the crypto-market.

Back to our story, you can, similarly to the stock market, divide coins in small cap, mid cap, and large cap based on the changes in the market capitalization. It should be clear that large cap are the more stable coins but the small caps can yield enormous rewards (often linked to enormous risk). While Bitcoin currently has the largest market capitalization, you can also look into smaller altcoins and consider what their future growth potential might be. Of course, you should also know that these charts don't guarantee what the future value of a cryptocurrency will be. You should look into the coins you want to invest in, analyze the supply and the underlying assumptions/technology before you make a final decision. The market cap also doesn't provide information considering the velocity of the cryptocurrency. Trends have to be analyzed over time. It's important to take into account the numerous allegations of crypto-market price manipulation.[43] Research shows systemic trends in Bitcoin price and the number of "large" participants in many altcoin markets, which means you need to scrutinize these investments even more closely.

Common appearances are wash trading (buying and selling with one's own funds to create the perception of market activity), pumps and dumps (artificial buying of an altcoin, after which you sell your stake to victims), dark pool trading (large trades outside of standard exchanges), shilling (generating false hype around a coin for personal gain), and whale trades (large investors pushing the price in their favor).[44] A final consideration when you look into overall market capitalization of the crypto-market is the existence of dead coins, which should be subtracted from the overall number (even though an exact number is unknown). Alternative approaches to performing deeper market analyses can be found in the corner of fundamental analysis.

[43]www.forbes.com/sites/billybambrough/2019/09/25/striking-bitcoin-research-points-to-price-manipulation/#4f9186665c2b
[44]https://hackernoon.com/the-mysterious-manipulation-of-crypto-markets-and-how-to-manage-5234e19e6e77

Crypto Futures Trading

For those of you who are interested: futures trading has also entered the world of cryptocurrencies. In December 2017, the Chicago Mercantile Exchange launched the first Bitcoin futures contract.[45] These futures were cash settled, meaning that at the end of the contract, one has to compare the current market value to the agreed upon price, after which there is a transfer of the value. These types of contracts are often used to smooth out the risk that an investor (or miner) has by holding a certain amount of a tokens (in this case Bitcoin). However, these can also be used by speculators who want to bet on the price movement of cryptocurrencies.

In a market where accusations of market manipulation already exist, you should take into account the extra risk you face by holding such contracts. Other criticism also refers to the fact that cash-delivered futures don't force investors to actually hold the altcoin in hand, which leads to the fear that this could lead to the dilution of the market supply. There are also physically delivered futures, such as those provided by Bakkt.[46] Upon settlement, there is a "physical" exchange of Bitcoin between the participants. Kraken has futures on Ethereum, Litecoin, Bitcoin Cash, Ripple, and Bitcoin.[47]

As this book does not focus on options trading, I will not go into the details of going short, long, and margin calls. All I can do is issue a warning for those who want to enter this type of market. It is a market that can provide liquidity and offer hedging instruments to existing positions, but it can also introduce a whole lot of risk if you speculate on future prices.[48] As with any market, it is always the same rule: know the market you are entering and understand the risks of the instruments that you are buying or selling. And even in that case, always do your due diligence.

Crypto Dividends

Throughout this book, I have shown that cryptocurrencies have been used and are being used in a similar way as "classic" investment instruments. They have been used in ICOs to raise money for startups, create digital twins and crypto-assets, and people have made money over mining and trading altcoins.[49]

---

[45]https://medium.com/scalar-capital/futures-crypto-8ac1a993ce85
[46]www.bakkt.com/index
[47]www.kraken.com/features/futures
[48]www.howtotoken.com/for-traders/trade-bitcoin-futures-ultimate-guide-part1/
[49]https://coinsutra.com/cryptocurrency-dividends/

However, some of these altcoins have implemented a new strategy for investors to make money: dividends. There are two ways you can start making dividends with cryptocurrencies:

- Staking: Holding a proof of stake coin in a special wallet
- Holding: Buying and holding an altcoin in a wallet

A first example of an altcoin paying dividends is Komodo (KMD), which can be staked in a staking wallet after you buy it. It promises a return of 5% on an annual basis. NEO is a smart contract token, similar to Ethereum, where you can stake your NEO in order to receive a payout in GAS.[50] VeChain uses the same mechanism as NEO, but instead of paying out GAS, it pays out VTHOR.

Another example is BTMX, which is the token of the BitMax exchange. You can lock up the coin to earn USDT (the reward is calculated and distributed daily). Kucoin (KCS) is an altcoin linked to the KuCoin exchange and distributes 50% of transaction fees to the token holders. The Coss token of the Coss Exchange has a similar mechanism in place.

Other interesting tokens are Pundi X, PIVX, and BiBox. The future will certainly show more altcoins with different payouts. If you are interested in such an investment, always make sure that you perform due diligence so that you understand both the dividend scheme as the risks involved.

Bonded Escrow Contract

Bonded escrow contracts are an area where blockchain smart contracts could effectively help optimize existing companies and the regulation in place.[51] These smart contracts could help eliminate the middleman for a lot of existing services, effectively making these processes more consumer friendly, cheaper, and in some cases safer. When we talk about escrow services, smart contracts could introduce the "safe remote purchase."[52] For those who do not know what escrow services are, they simply relate to a trusted third-party when you are dealing with an untrusted relationship between buyers and sellers. An example is one of the many online platforms that handle second hand merchandising. If you sell a product on such a platform, you generally don't know the buyer, so how can you make sure that you get your money when you send the product? And vice versa, how does the buyer know that they will receive the product when they pay the seller?

---

[50]www.bestcryptodividends.com/

[51]https://hackernoon.com/how-a-smart-contract-replaced-an-escrow-company-in-a-60k-deal-551ff7839044

[52]https://medium.com/coinmonks/escrow-service-as-a-smart-contract-the-business-logic-5b678ebe1955

The escrow service locks in the payment of the buyer and only releases the payment to the seller when the buyer confirms that they received the product. This happens for a fee of course.

Instead of an escrow service, consider a smart contract. The code can vary depending on the use case, but it will generally force both the seller and the buyer to put up a stake so that they both have incentive to follow the stipulations of the agreement. When one of them doesn't follow the rules of the agreement, the code of the smart contract will penalize that participant and they will lose their stake. This not only reduces the cost for the participants (as you generally don't have to pay for a smart contract, and if you have to it will be significantly less than what you currently pay for an escrow service), but it also ensures that the participants follow the rules.

Double-Betting Strategy

The double-betting strategy is a mining strategy that has been pre-programmed in the Satoshi reference miner.[53] This means that if a miner discovers a block and at the same time another miner discovers a competing block, the miner will not simply switch to the other block. Instead they will keep on mining on their own chain. This because neither of the miners knows which of the two blocks will be the one that the majority of the miners continuing mining.

You can understand that this is not the most optimal way of working, as hashing power and energy are lost when mining several blocks at the same time and when other miners are building on top of conflicting chains. To solve this issue, several algorithms have been proposed, such as DECOR and GHOST+DECOR.

Token Curated Registry

Token Curated Registries are a building block of decentralized applications based on fungible tokens and digital scarcity.[54] Two examples of such registries are the adChain registry, which keeps a cryptographically secure record of publisher domain names, and Messari.[55,56]

adChain and other registries are listings generated by token holders and these can be anything from hash records to actual detailed records stored in IPFS. The TCR is used to serve as an identity mechanism, which allows advertisers to know something about listed participants without having

---

[53]https://bitslog.com/2014/05/02/decor/
[54]https://hackernoon.com/token-curated-registry-tcr-design-patterns-4de6d18efa15
[55]https://messari.io/
[56]https://publisher.adchain.com/

previous relations with them and exclude fraudulent participants that would like to take advantage.[57] How do participants become part of the whitelist? They can submit a deposit to become part of the whitelist, after which a challenge period starts. During this challenge period, existing participants can challenge the newcomer and post an equivalent amount against the deposit of the newcomer. In this case, a voting period starts where all the other members of the whitelist can vote on the issue. If the challenger succeeds, they receive special dispensations on top of their own deposit and all the other voters that voted in their favor receive a piece of the newcomers deposit as well (who will not become a member in this case). If the newcomer wins, they receive their deposit back and can eventually become a member. Of course, members can be challenged any point in time if evidence of fraudulent behavior arises. Changes in the deposit requirements of a TCR can lead to the removal of participants if they don't comply.

You can see that this system helps create some kind of quality label in a decentralized world. Does this mean that TCRs are a flawless system? Of course not, as these implementations have run into some criticism as well.[58] Aleksandr Bulkin cites the example of blockchain oracles, which do work in his opinion opposite to TCRs. The reason is that oracles require people to bet on (easily) publicly observable information in which honest players are rewarded and dishonest players lose their stakes. Getting the majority of the participants to vote for the wrong answer is incredibly hard, nearly impossible. The key components of the oracle is that there is objective information that can publicly be observed at a low cost. From the moment that this information is no longer publicly available or that there is a considerable cost to verify this information, the participants can be manipulated to no longer support the correct answers. When we extrapolate this logic to TCRs, which are in place to collect and verify information that is difficult to ascertain, we know that there are possible issues with the economic incentives. So, depending on the environment the TCR operates in, it will either be very successful or will fail to bring the certainty that participants in the decentralized network are looking for.

Some Final Remarks

I hope you found this book to be an interesting resource in the world of blockchain technology and development. I tried to provide a first guide, which means that I wasn't able to explain all concepts, frameworks, and networks in detail. Each of these topics deserves (and often has) complete books of its own.

---

[57] https://medium.com/@simondlr/city-walls-bo-taoshi-exploring-the-power-of-token-curated-registries-588f208c17d5

[58] https://blog.coinfund.io/curate-this-token-curated-registries-that-dont-work-d76370b77150

My goal was to introduce these concepts so that, based on your interest, you can explore them further. The Internet is filled with free resources that allow you to learn more, but there are also numerous courses and books that give you more insight into these topics. Websites such as Hackernoon.com, medium. com, and blockgeeks.com offer tons of information that can help you even better understand the world of blockchain and cryptocurrencies.

A second remark that I want to make concerns the fact that this is almost a "historic" artifact. This means that the second I finished this book, there were already certain points that were outdated. An example is the Ethereum network future development plan that is open to change and has already changed. This means that historic information is exactly that. In the same vein, I apologize for the errata in this book. I wrote this with a lot of enthusiasm, but I am sure that there are certain mistakes that I missed and were left behind.

Finally, I would like to add that I am honored you chose to read my book. Thank you for being my reader. If you would like to be in contact, don't hesitate to connect on LinkedIn or visit my website at www.stijnvanhijfte.com.

Index

© Stijn Van Hijfte 2020
S. Van Hijfte, *Decoding Blockchain for Business*,
https://doi.org/10.1007/978-1-4842-6137-8

Printed in the United States
By Bookmasters